The Body
Burning Detail

The Body Burning Detail

Memoir of a Marine Artilleryman in Vietnam

BILL JONES

Foreword by VESS QUINLAN

McFarland & Company, Inc., Publishers

Jefferson, North Carolina

ISBN (print) 978-1-4766-7517-6 ∞
ISBN (ebook) 978-1-4766-3424-1

LIBRARY OF CONGRESS CATALOGUING DATA ARE AVAILABLE

BRITISH LIBRARY CATALOGUING DATA ARE AVAILABLE

Front cover: Author in Firebase Neville in Quảng Trị Province,
Vietnam, in December, 1968

Printed in the United States of America

*McFarland & Company, Inc., Publishers
Box 611, Jefferson, North Carolina 28640
www.mcfarlandpub.com*

To Gloria

Artillery lends dignity to what might otherwise be a vulgar brawl.—Frederick the Great

If you don't have enough artillery, quit.—General Richard Carsasas, U.S. Army, 1951–1984

TABLE OF CONTENTS

Table of Contents

Table of Contents

ACKNOWLEDGMENTS

There are a lot of people to thank whenever anyone completes the process of writing a book. "The Body Burning Detail" is certainly no exception. So, upfront, my sincere and humble apologies to whomever I have left unthanked. You know who you are.

First, the nice folks at the Western Folklife Center in Elko, Nevada, financed my way to the National Cowboy Poetry Gathering many years ago to recite some poems. Not once, but several times. It was a life-changing experience and the friends I made there were (and are) both cherished and invaluable. I still go to the gatherings, some thirty years later, but fortunately I can pay my own way now.

Vess Quinlan, an early supporter, accomplished and gifted poet, author, rancher, political observer, philosopher and all-around nice guy, has been a great and loyal friend from the early days. Without his encouragement, advice and suggestions I would have never attempted writing a book about the Vietnam War in the first place.

John Dofflemeyer is a California rancher, blogster, poet and editor of the Dry Crik Review. Twenty-five years ago he published "Blood Trails," a collection of war poems by me and another Viet vet, Rod McQueary. It was a risky venture, both financially and otherwise. (There is, by the way, not a lot of money in publishing poetry books. Or most other books either.) In addition, many in the cowboy-poetry genre were of the opinion that war poems have no place in the cowboy, western, livestock industry subculture. John, a talented free-verse maverick who rarely succumbs to unsolicited advice from anyone, said in response, "Cowboys go to war too." In many ways, he is indirectly responsible for "The Body Burning Detail." Any unfavorable criticism of the book should go directly to him.

Rod McQueary, my friend and co-author of "Blood Trails," another former Marine living in the shadow of the Vietnam War, left us much too

Acknowledgments

soon. I wish he was here and could read this book, as he would give me an honest, thoughtful evaluation of its strengths, weaknesses and readability. "Be anything but boring," Rod would say. And he was never boring. I miss Rod and his rambling late-night phone calls, advice, bullshit and unconditional friendship.

Bill Sniffin, editor and publisher of the Wyoming State Journal as well as many other publications, was kind enough to print my weekly columns for several years. A lot of them, quite frankly, were not works of great literature, but I had a lot of fun and generated a lot of irate letters to the editor. Satire and irony, I learned quickly enough, are concepts foreign to a majority of the newspaper-reading public. Perhaps Bill was only looking for "filler" articles for his paper, but he paid me (not much, by the way, but no doubt more than the columns were worth) and that gave me the confidence to continue trying to put something entertaining or marginally significant on paper. Bill took a chance on me, an inexperienced and unknown wannabe writer, and I am forever grateful.

C. J. Hadley, editor and publisher of *RANGE* magazine, may well be one of the most interesting and unique women I have ever known. A fugitive from Great Britain, she is an early fan and believer in "The Body Burning Detail." A little blonde whirling dervish of limitless energy spouting entertaining and outlandish stories (all of which are true ... no one could make them up), she generously shares her lifetime of experience in writing and publishing. She will occasionally publish one of my "rants" or poems in her magazine or award-winning books. Thanks, CJ. *You* need to write a book.

Denyse Pellettieri White, my proofreader/editor, has put a lot of work into this project. Although I have never met her in person, over many phone calls and emails we have developed a most pleasant relationship based on mutual respect and a common interest—which was to get this book in shape for the publisher. She is the very best at what she does and is a super nice person. Not only that, but Denyse says she really likes the book. Could any author ask for more? Without her there would be no book and my gratitude ... well, I don't have a proper adjective for it.

There is also the United States Marine Corps. I never liked the Marine Corps all that much. And I was far from a model Marine the two short years I was a part of it. But I loved those young Marines with whom I served. Most of them, anyway. Once a Marine, always a Marine. Trite and a tad corny perhaps, but nevertheless true enough.

Acknowledgments

Then there is my biggest fan, confidant, partner in crime, gentle critic, and wife extraordinaire Gloria H. Jones, who reads everything I write and (almost always) likes me anyway. It has been a forty-plus year adventure, an interesting and delightful ride that is passing far too quickly. I wish we could do it all again...

I could go on with many more names. Hundreds, maybe. But you probably would not know any of them. And invariably I would leave someone important out. Plus, it would be boring.

Foreword
by Vess Quinlan

If you only read one book about the Vietnam War, it should be this one. It is not a dry-as-cornflakes tale of strategy or tactics. With great writing and superb storytelling skill, Bill Jones takes you through Marine boot camp where experts deflate excess self-esteem and strip a group of young men consisting of mostly college dropouts, sons of poor fathers, assorted minorities, and miscellaneous hoodlums down to only bone and muscle, then rebuild these boys into men trained, equipped, and determined to be your best friends or your worst enemies. Otherwise known as U.S. Marines.

Imagine finding yourself in a hole scooped out of the red soil of Vietnam, wet, cold and scared to death, with another Marine who is just as wet, cold and scared as you are. Imagine thinking that your survival could well depend on this fellow Marine and knowing that in your former life, when driving through his neighborhood, you would be sure to lock your car doors.

This book is about going weeks without a shower, a change of clothes, or a hot meal. About how strangers became closer than family as they went where they were sent and did what they were told to do, often without knowing where they were or exactly where the orders came from. Some of the events are laugh-out-loud funny, or as bawdy as young men can make them, and others are heart wrenching and sad.

Bill's father served in the Second World War—"the last good war"— and troops came home to parades and cheering crowds. The troops from Bill's war came home to jeers and insults from some of the clueless student-deferment crowd. The unintended or perhaps fully intended consequences of providing deferments to the sons of the rich and connected or the academically gifted created a nasty division in our society that exists to this very day.

Race or social position did not matter here. They were Marines. When Bill says they were the finest people he ever knew, he means it.

Vess Quinlan, a Colorado rancher, poet and writer whose father and several uncles returned from the Pacific after World War II. A member of the board of trustees for the Western Folklife Center, Quinlan recently has been involved in promoting the Veterans History Project sponsored by the Library of Congress.

THE BODY BURNING DETAIL

Three soldiers from the North
burned for reasons
of sanitation.
Arms shrunk to seal flippers
charred buttocks thrust skyward
they burn for five days.
It is hard to swallow
difficult to eat
with the sweet smoke of seared
flesh, like fog,
everywhere.

Twenty-five years later
they burn still.
Across seas of time
the faint unwelcome odor
rises in odd places.
With a load of leaves
at the city dump
a floating wisp of smoke
from the burning soldiers
mingles with the stench
of household garbage.

Once, while watching young boys
kick a soccer ball,
the Death Smell fills my lungs.
As I run, choking
panic unfolds
fluttering wings
of fear and remorse.
A narrow escape...

A letter, snatched from flames
the day we burned them,
is hidden away
in a shoebox
with gag birthday cards,
buttons, string, rubber bands.
A letter from home?
The Oriental words,
delicately formed,
are still a mystery...

PREFACE

Why attempt to write a memoir in the first place? Is it self-indulgent? An attempt to put our individual spin on past history? A need to exorcize some demons/angels lurking in our fading memories? Perhaps it is all of these. Or maybe it is none, but just a desire to tell a story, part of the human condition that otherwise would be lost forever.

At the time, like probably most Marines, I had a love/hate relationship with the Corps. Nevertheless, despite some misgivings, I reluctantly went wherever they sent me and once I got there I did whatever they told me to do. "The Body Burning Detail" has its beginnings as a poem written over thirty years ago—later published in a book of war poems entitled "Blood Trails," written with my late friend and Marine Vietnam veteran Rod McQueary. Many of the poems have been subsequently published in a number of books and anthologies. (*People* magazine wrote that the book is "stunning and poignant." I had to look up the word "poignant" as I had no idea what it meant.)

I was not a "grunt" (infantry), and compared to many I did not see much actual combat—although I saw all I wanted. Actually, a lot more than I wanted. But I often think of the war and my fellow Marines almost daily, mostly in fleeting flashes of colorful and indelible images. The war is part of me now. And, perhaps even more importantly, it is also a part of us.

This story is not necessarily in any particular sequence. Like the war itself, the events described are chaotic, confusing and somewhat difficult to categorize. I could not put them in order even if I tried. Names have been forgotten or changed, conversations recreated from memory, locations inadvertently switched, military operations and procedures no doubt sometimes inaccurately described. If some of the profanity is offensive, well ... perhaps you should be even more offended by the war itself. War,

5

by its very nature, is the most obscene and offensive thing I can think of ... with the possible exception of a political system that involves young men in unwinnable, dubious conflicts from which the rich and powerful are shielded. In the next war, everyone's kids need to serve—or at least be at risk. But I digress...

The Vietnam War was not fought by the elite and privileged of our society. General Westmoreland stated that it was fought by "the poor man's sons." For the most part, we were the offspring of blue collar workers, African Americans, Native Americans, Hispanics, the poor and politically powerless, the disadvantaged and marginalized, the undereducated, and the unsophisticated, most of whom were struggling on the bottom rungs of the socioeconomic ladder. Unlike so many of those who sidestepped military service with college deferments, our ranks were populated by high school and college dropouts. Some, probably a lot more than you think, had become involved with our court system. Military service was sometimes a substitute for jail. Those not drafted often enlisted because they simply had no other viable employment alternatives. Others thought, erroneously it seems now, that their patriotic service and sacrifice would be honored and rewarded. All were an expendable and insignificant element of our country's youth, some might say, especially those in power responsible for waging and losing America's longest and most divisive war.

These proud and profane young Marines, from such varied and often-troubled backgrounds, would do anything for one another, including risking and even sacrificing their very lives. The willingness with which many of them went, sometimes almost eagerly, to their deaths is something that will remain with me forever.

They were, without question, the finest people I ever met.

1

PACK YOUR TRASH

"It is not what you know for sure that gets you in trouble. It is what you know for sure that just ain't so."—Mark Twain

If you are a student of military strategy and tactics this book probably is not for you. If you are looking for a Hollywood combat adventure story, the same applies. "Rambo" exists only in the movies. (Sylvester Stallone, who plays Rambo, taught at a girl's school in France during the Vietnam War to avoid the draft.) This story, my story, is by an unsophisticated twenty-year-old Marine draftee who most of the time had no idea even where he *was* in Vietnam. Unlike Rambo, I did nothing especially heroic and lived simply day to day—a lot of the time scared shitless. Nevertheless, the eleven months and twenty-five days I spent in Vietnam remains the most influential and significant period of my life. And I feel somewhat compelled to write it down for a variety of reasons, none of which are entirely clear.

In the summer of 1968 the United States' military tactics in Vietnam change from "take and hold" to a more mobile concept of "search and destroy." I was initially assigned to a battery of artillery with the 3rd Battalion, 12th Marine Regiment, 3rd Marine Division. Operations are confined to "I Corps," a region just south of the demilitarized zone. The DMZ. Artillery firebases are established along the southern edges of the DMZ to prevent the flow of troops and supplies from North Vietnam and to provide support for our own infantry. Did this strategy work? Well, maybe on a temporary basis. But long term, none of our tactics appear to have been successful, and, almost fifty-nine thousand American lives later, Vietnam is one united Communist country. As a people and country, did we learn anything? I will leave that up to you...

There were almost two different wars going on in Vietnam. One in the southern part of the country and another uniquely different one along

7

the DMZ. The firebases are isolated and supplied solely by helicopter. Living conditions are wretched and during my entire tour I have virtually no contact with Vietnamese civilians. Those assigned to rear areas have a different experience altogether than those unfortunate troops relegated to the "bush." If you are infantry, no matter where you are assigned, your life is pretty much miserable. I was not infantry (thank God), but I was not a rear-area guy either. Memories exist in a fog—sometimes a mere mist and other times impenetrable—and often make liars of us all. Is my story entirely factual? Probably not. For example, on the Internet I learned through a military "after action" report, that an event I thought was true was not really accurate. A helicopter shot down at LZ Argonne did not kill everyone, as I believed. Only the pilot was killed. The crew fought off the NVA and was later rescued. I learned this forty years after the fact.

Other incidents have morphed into a surreal, dreamlike quality. Did that really happen? A couple of times in Vietnam I had the sensation that events were not really happening at all, but that I was watching myself in a movie. Crazy, perhaps, until I discovered that this was a fairly common "out of body" type experience involving life-threatening circumstances. All wars are basically the same. All war stories share a common element. At least the true ones. This story is as true as I can make it.

On television I watch military commanders in Iraq and Afghanistan brief troops prior to an operation: We are going here or there. Our objective is this or that. We will be supported by the following units... We expect these things to happen, et cetera. In Vietnam, nobody told me, a lowly lance corporal, anything but "Pack your trash, we are leaving right away." I suppose the officers and NCO's were briefed, but I never really knew where we were going. Or cared, for that matter.

If anyone wants to know how a war is progressing there is one surefire way to find out. Find the lowest-level enlisted man (one who is in harm's way, preferably a grunt) and ask him. With nothing to lose, he will usually be more truthful than anyone. A general? A politician? Not so much.

So if any of this appeals to you, read on. Pack your trash, we are leaving right away.

2

WE DON'T WANT
ANY CANDY ASSES

*"I had other priorities."—Secretary of Defense Richard "Dick" Cheney
explaining his five student draft deferments*

"From my work I came to believe the draft system itself is illegitimate."—President Bill Clinton

In the mid–1960s military recruiters roam the hallways of America in search of young men needed to fight in our country's rapidly expanding misadventure in Vietnam. During that time high school authorities commonly allowed the recruiters free and unfettered access to male students, permitting them to entice, cajole, encourage and often deceive virtually anyone with a pulse to enlist. Their efforts are aided by the "draft" (involuntary conscription) that hangs like an anvil suspended by a thread over the heads of all male Baby Boomers. Without a college deferment or severe medical condition, a letter from the county Selective Service Board is inevitable. National Guard and Reserve units, neither of which is normally deployed to Southeast Asia, are at full strength with those avoiding service in "Rice Paddy Land." Without some connection to our political elite it is nearly impossible to join either of them. The waiting list is rumored to be two years long.

In the spring of 1965, a Marine recruiter stands before a South Carolina high school auditorium of junior and senior boys. Attendance is mandatory. The Marine's speech is in stark contrast to the pitch of Navy and Air Force recruiters, both of whom dangle the promise of technical skills and easy living. The Marine sergeant, resplendent in dress blues and with several rows of ribbons, eyes the assembled adolescents warily. I detect a certain amount of arrogant, thinly disguised contempt. The presentation is short. It contains no promises.

9

"We don't want any candy asses," the recruiter says. "If you are a candy ass do not even attempt to talk to me."

That is the entire recruitment speech. Nothing more. To a couple of hundred testosterone-challenged teenage boys, nothing could have been more effective. At this time the Vietnam War is only beginning to sour and America's opinion of our involvement has yet to descend from disenchantment to disillusionment to widespread, outright opposition. We can still see "the light at the end of the tunnel." Years later, much too late, we learn there is no light. Furthermore, there probably never was a light or a tunnel.

Two boys from my high school enlist in the Marines that day—or at least start the process. One of them, Leland "Mac" Hammond, is a year older than me. I know him slightly. Both boys posture and strut in the halls, reveling in their newfound status as potential heroes. In those days, joining the Marines means you are going to war.

A year or so later, prior to flunking out of college, I am in a local drugstore and see Mac's picture in *Life* magazine. Mac is in Vietnam and four of his fellow Marines, their faces anguished and determined, are dragging his lifeless body through tall grass. The photograph, by the famous journalist Larry Burrows, becomes one of the iconic images of the Vietnam War. Reprinted countless times, it is displayed at the Marine Corps Museum in Quantico, Virginia. Larry Burrows is killed in Vietnam some five years after taking the photo. In my mind, the picture is as clear to me today as the first time I saw it.

Some fifty years later, via the Internet, I learn the details of Mac Hammond's death in Vietnam. His unit is in a running firefight along the DMZ in Quang Tri Province during Operation Prairie. Mac is a lance corporal fire team leader with 2nd Battalion, 5th Marine Regiment, 3rd Marine Division. One of his friends, who attempts to save the severely wounded Mac, tells of that day, October 11, 1966:

"I knew he had a collapsed lung so I slapped a bandage on and started mouth-to-mouth. I could feel he was dying and couldn't figure out why. Later I realize when he took the first round it spun him round and he took another one under his right arm. There was no saving him."

As the Marines carry the body of nineteen-year-old Mac to an evacuation helicopter, a deck of cards, with Mac's lucky ace of spades facing out, slips from his pocket. Mac had lost six dollars the night before to one of the Marines carrying him. The three-month-long Operation Prairie cost the lives of Mac and some two hundred others, wounding well over one thousand. The North Vietnamese Army allegedly lost 1,329 killed. Although I believe in the accuracy of the Marine casualties, I have doubts about the number of enemy killed in action. Based on my later experience, I venture to speculate it is a wild-ass guess.

A year or so after Mac's death, as a result of my less-than-stellar college performance, a letter arrives from the local draft board. "Greetings," it says on behalf of the president, "you have been selected...." The University of South Carolina, I learn later, has sent my school records to the local draft board. Although my grades are not that bad, the board determines that I am "not making sufficient progress toward a degree." My decision to drop a couple of math and science courses, I conclude much too late, was probably a serious error in judgment.

Soon I am standing essentially naked with three hundred other "selectees" at the military processing center at Fort Jackson, South Carolina. A bag containing our valuables hangs by a string around our necks. During the genital exam, it is discovered the guy standing next to me has three testicles. Other than being a source of amusement and curiosity to the Army medics, he is nonetheless approved for military service. It is my impression that nearly everyone—unless you are a hopeless cripple with documentation—will pass this sham physical.

The Vietnam War is escalating and America's military is in desperate need of more bodies to fuel its burgeoning war machine. The Huntley/Brinkley Nightly News brings the casualty figures to our living rooms daily: "Four hundred killed in action this week." Another week the number exceeds five hundred. This particular month, April 1968, forty-eight thousand men are conscripted into military service. Since young men are not exactly lining up at the Marine Recruitment Office to voluntarily enlist, forty-three hundred of this group are going to the Marines. Probably kicking and screaming, but going nevertheless. During the Vietnam War some forty-three thousand draftees are delegated to the Marine Corps.

At the induction and reception center, a Marine sergeant is picking one or two guys from each group to leave for Marine recruit training ... that day. The draftees look stunned. Like me, they think they are going into the Army. No one told them Marines sometimes were drafted. In the Army, at least there is a chance you will be sent to Germany or Korea. Almost always, Marines go to Vietnam. Usually as infantry. The "tip of the spear."

The Body Burning Detail

The little group of future Marines, the "chosen ones," is eyed by everyone else with awe. And perhaps something that resembles sympathy. There is something going on that is difficult to explain. A mystique surrounds the Marine Corps and (whatever it is) it is evident here. The Marine sergeant shakes his head knowingly and smiles at the shocked little gaggle of recruits headed for Marine boot camp.

"I need two more," the sergeant announces. "Any volunteers?"

Two hands are timidly raised. One of them, for reasons I still don't fully understand, is mine.

Nobody is more surprised than me.

3

I Can't Hear You!

"Back in the old Corps, we weren't training those privates to infiltrate into the peacetime Marine Corps. We were training those privates to go to Vietnam."—R. Lee Ermey, Marine Drill Instructor

The brainwashing at Marine boot camp begins early. Two hundred years in the making, the techniques have been honed to a sharpness unparalleled by any other military organization. It is an unforgettable, unique, life-changing event that few ever forget or want to repeat. A bus load of recruits, including me and at least a couple more draftees, arrive at Parris Island, South Carolina, in the dead of night. (I later learn this is all by design.) Decades later, it is amazing how much of the experience, in detail, I can still recall. For example, I can still remember verbatim the speech a drill instructor gave to us at 2:00 a.m., April 19, 1968:

"On behalf of the president of the United States, the secretary of the Navy and the commandant of the Marine Corps, I would like to welcome you assholes to Recruit Training Depot, Parris Island. The smoking lamp is out. If you have any chewing gum in your mouth, swallow it." (A big wad of Double Bubble sticks in my throat and I nearly choke myself out.) "From this moment on, the first and last words out of your scuzzy pieholes will be SIR. For example: 'SIR, the private is a shit-bird.' 'SIR, the private is a worthless scumbag, SIR.' You are *not* Marines. From the looks of you, none of you will *ever* be Marines. I can't believe the recruiters are sending me this worthless trash. When I give you the word, and only when I give the word, I want you to get all your personal gear, and moving as quickly as humanly possible, get the fuck off this bus. You will then assume the position of attention on the yellow footprints. You have exactly three seconds—I repeat, three motherfucking seconds—to accomplish this task. Two of those seconds are already gone. *DO IT!*"

The Body Burning Detail

Already I am thinking perhaps raising my hand back at Fort Jackson may very well have been the monumental mistake of the century...

People are now running over one another and trying to jump out of windows. In retrospect, if we had any sense we would have stayed on the bus. Things gets infinitely worse and rapidly proceed downhill. Two other drill instructors, hands on hips, wait outside and make the first drill instructor seem like a friendly and smiling Mr. Rogers. There is lots of screaming and yelling and "I CAN'T HEAR YOU!" Any question not answered at full volume is unacceptable. In the first two hours, I get slapped three times: for moving too slow, for not following instructions, and for "eyeballing the motherfucking area." Perhaps, I think wistfully, these are not really drill instructors, but are three escapees from a local asylum who stole uniforms from the supply warehouse and just happened to be walking by when our bus arrives. The real drill instructors will soon arrive and deal with these bat-shit crazy, certified insane imposters. Hope springs eternal...

It is all finely orchestrated to gain control through intimidation. And it is pretty effective with a bunch of eighteen- and nineteen-year-old kids. The cursing (which I understand is not even allowed anymore) is inventive, creative, colorful, and without precedent. At least to those of us raised with primarily conservative, fundamentalist religious backgrounds. I never heard, before or since, such outrageous profanity. One phrase, which has stuck with me for over forty years, concerns a young kid who had a moderately long "hippy" haircut before being unceremoniously shorn bald. Much to his immediate regret, he glances sidelong at the drill instructor. Big mistake. "What are you looking at, you long-haired, pot-smoking, peter-puffing, sandal-footed motherfucker? I'll come over there and...." This is cursing elevated to a poetic art form. And as a result, even to this day, I am seldom shocked or offended by almost any profanity. After hearing it eloquently spewed nonstop by accomplished and professional experts, the words ultimately lose their power. Especially when attempted by civilian amateurs.

Our platoon consists of Mexican Americans, black kids, and the sons of working-class, blue collar Americans. There are a few fellow college flunkies and one kid who has just washed out of Officer Candidate School. (The drill instructors, once they find out he at one time wanted to be an officer, make the poor kid's life a living, constant hell on earth.) An African American youth on the top bunk directly over my rack confides in me that he has trouble sleeping at night. The anticipation of a decent breakfast the next morning keeps him awake. Never, he says, has he eaten such good food; never has he had enough to eat. By the end of boot camp he blossoms into a fit and muscled young bull. If there are any kids in boot camp from well-to-do families, I never meet any. Many are recruited from city and county lockups and given the choice: Marine Corps or stay in jail. Some will openly declare, after a couple of days at Parris Island, that they made the wrong decision.

Marine recruits during boot camp are continually supervised by sergeant drill instructors. Usually three of them—sergeants, staff sergeants, and gunnery sergeants. Twenty-four hours of every day. Seven days a week. The senior sergeant is in charge and assumes the role as kind of a "father figure"—although a strict and demanding one. By the end of recruit training, members of the platoon would unhesitatingly run through the closed, burning gates of hell (setting ourselves on fire in the process) for a half-assed word of praise from the senior drill instructor. Once, he suggests, "We almost look like real Marines." Our spirits soar and we march and strut with renewed purpose and vigor.

One of the remaining two drill instructors is known as the "heavy hat"—the platoon disciplinarian. Usually, he maintains a persona that can be best described as leaning towards borderline insanity. To me, he always seems dangerously close to a homicidal rage. At the time (1968), Marine recruits wore helmet liners sprayed with silver paint, called "chrome domes." Sometimes my platoon's heavy would carry a little ball-peen hammer and bop offending recruits on the helmets with it. It does not hurt, but does get your undivided and immediate attention. It should be noted that among all the drill instructors their individual roles sometimes can reverse ... in an instant. The "nice" drill instructor can morph magically into a raving maniac and the "heavy" then transforms into your best friend and buddy. This bizarre manipulation scenario keeps us somewhat confused, paranoid, willing to be controlled, and anxious to please those in authority. Group punishment is liberally used and is highly effective. One recruit screws up and the entire platoon is punished. You are only as strong, the drill instructors say, as your weakest link. Learn to work together or you die together.

R. Lee Ermy, a former drill instructor, several years ago is originally hired to be the technical advisor for the boot camp scenes in the movie "Full Metal Jacket." A Vietnam War classic loosely based on the battle for the city of Hue, the boot camp activities at the beginning are extremely realistic and bring back an avalanche of memories. Mr. Ermy is given complete freedom to invent dialogue, adlib and even alter the script in these scenes as he sees fit—an unprecedented event in the movie industry. Although he does not have a lot of acting experience, he is ultimately hired to play the foul-mouthed drill instructor in the film. A regular actor, even an accomplished one, is just not believable in the role. Ermy receives an Academy Award for Best Supporting Actor. Realistically, he is not acting at all, but is simply recreating his days as a Marine Corps drill instructor. It is an outstanding performance and an honest portrayal of Marine boot camp during the Vietnam era. Almost any drill instructor—at least all the ones with which I am familiar—could have assumed the role just as easily. All they would need to do is act normal...

After seven weeks, the platoon is assigned to a week of "mess duty" and issued white mess-hall type clothing. This duty consists of long hours of drudge work: washing pots, peeling potatoes, swabbing the decks and assisting the cooks. But there is a bonus—a pretty big one. We are now away from the watchful eyes of the drill instructors. We get all we want to eat. Sometimes the cooks, regular Marines, give us a few minutes' break. It is a vacation of sorts. Our senior drill instructor marches us back to the barracks at night. Standing at attention in front of our racks one evening, I can tell he is not pleased. This is another speech that is hot branded forever in my memory:

"I saw you ladies at the chow hall today. Had a real good time, didn't you? An undisciplined mob! I have never been so embarrassed." (We live in fear of "embarrassing" the senior drill instructor.) "Smoking ... joking ... eyeballing the area ... talking to the mess cooks like they were your motherfucking drinking buddies ... finger fucking the chow...." (I still don't know what he means by that.) "You girls are going to pay. Bends and Thrusts!" (This is a particularly detestable exercise also known as "Bends and Motherfuckers.") "Many, many of them. Ready ... begin!" His goal, he says, after about an hour, is to "melt you hogs down into a little pile of hair and fingernails." He almost succeeds.

Private Lane, a black former gang member from Los Angeles, is standing next to me during this Inquisition. Like me, he has gorged himself on brownies and ice cream at the evening meal. It is unbearably hot and he is going to be sick, but he first asks the senior drill instructor for permission to throw up. "Go ahead, Lane," our senior says. "But stay in the position of attention."

16

3. I Can't Hear You!

Lane projectile vomits a couple of times into the middle of the squad bay. The rest of us, although grateful for the rest, are busy quelling our own propensity to follow suit. My own brownies and ice cream are on the verge of escaping and joining Lane's on the squad-bay deck. "Sir," Lane says, "the private is finished puking, Sir!" Told to clean it up, Lane scurries off to get a swab (mop) from the rack downstairs. The cleaning job is hurried and not very thorough.

"Lane, when you put that swab back on the rack," the senior asks, "did you bother to wash it out?" I catch a glimpse of Lane in the corner of my eye. I know he didn't wash it out. He wasn't down there that long. Lane is now in a quandary. He can say "no" and pay the consequences or lie and say "yes" and hope nobody checks. "Yes, Sir!" Lane counters. "Private Lane rinsed out the swab!" (Private Lane, like the rest of us, always refers to himself in the third person. Saying "I" is an offense severely punished. Neither is "you" permitted, as "ewe" is a female sheep.)

"Great," our senior replies. "Glad to hear it. You are going to wear that swab for the next two days."

Later, I see Lane in the mess hall, wearing the mop head like a wig. It still has chunks of vomit in it.

He is sitting at a table all by himself...

LIGHTS OUT

After taps and prayers
("Goodnight Chesty Puller
wherever you are")
Drill Instructor Martinez struts
between rows of double racks
delivering scuttlebutt and sermonettes.

"You girls done good today.
But don't get too 'salty.'
You are still a herd of fuckups.
And you best get your 'sheet' together
most ricky-tick.
Every Swingin' Dick here
is WestPac bound.
Six months from now
half you ladies
will be dead."

4.

BREATHE. RELAX. AIM.
SIGHT. SQUEEZE.

Rules for a gunfight:
1. Bring a gun.
2. Preferably, bring two guns.
3. Bring all your friends who have guns.
　　　　　　　　—U.S. Marine policy

The Marines claim it trains the best rifle marksmen in the world. I have little doubt this is true, as in boot camp the fundamentals of rifle marksmanship are pounded into you—both physically and mentally. Marine recruits spend two weeks at the rifle range after the first few weeks of training. The first week is spent "snapping in" without live ammunition. We learn about sight picture and shooting positions—sitting, kneeling, standing and prone. Some of these positions are awkward and painful. Kind of like yoga. An acronym used by the instructors has stayed with me for fifty years. B.R.A.S.S. Breathe. Relax. Aim. Sight. Squeeeeeeze...

"Listen up, Girls," the marksmanship instructor is saying to our assembled platoon, "this is important. Qualification day will be here before you know it. You *will* qualify if you do exactly what we say. Now remember, once you get a good stable position and get a good front sight picture, what do you do?"

We yell in unison: "Breathe! Relax! Aim! Sight! Squeeze!" By now we know the drill. We are Pavlov's dogs responding to the bell of our masters.

"I don't want anyone *jerking* the trigger," he continues. "Say, for example, you are out of boot camp and on liberty in nearby Beaufort." The mere possibility of this fills us with hope and gets our rapt and undivided attention. "You meet a good-looking young woman with the nicest set of tits you ever saw. One thing leads to another and soon you are fooling around. Do you reach up like a stripe-ass ape and start jerking on them tits?"

"No, Sir!" we respond heartily.

"What do you do then?"

"SQUEEZE," we bellow. "SQUEEZE."

Qualification day comes at the end of the second week. We spend half days that week pulling and marking targets and the other half shooting with live ammunition. Working the targets seems a little dangerous at first as the rounds are passing a few feet over our heads, but we are protected by a berm and it is reasonably safe. Years later I hear that the son of a famous person is killed working the targets by a ricochet bullet, but hundreds of thousands of Marine recruits have been through rifle training with few incidents.

One afternoon we are standing in formation and I am fiddling around with some gear and holding my M-14 rifle between my legs to leave both hands free. Suddenly I hear a rifle clatter to the ground. Someone, I think, is in a world of shit. Looking around I discover the rifle is ... mine. The rangemaster attacks with the speed of a wolf just spotting a crippled calf. "I am kicking you off my range," he rages, "and I am not one to issue idle threats. Go back to the barracks, pack your trash, and report to the range down the road."

I spend the rest of the afternoon, with a sea bag and all my gear, going from one rifle range to another. Nobody wants me because I am now, according to the other rangemasters, a "general fuckup." At the end of the day I return to the original range and am unceremoniously accepted back in the platoon. Obviously, this whole sham sideshow is for the benefit of the other recruits. Nevertheless, I never drop my rifle again. Nobody else does either.

On qualification day, despite my best efforts to use the tit-squeezing method, I am still "jerking" the trigger. This throws off any hope of accuracy and is a precursor to "Unq" status. Unqualified—a fate worse than death. Those who do not qualify on the rifle range are sent back to another platoon to start over. This potential development is simply too horrible to even consider. A range "coach," assigned to every two recruits on the firing line, has the perfect solution. "Give me your trigger finger," he says. "Now lay it on this cement block." He then takes a M-14 metal magazine and smashes the end of my finger. My index finger is so sore I can't do anything *but* squeeze the trigger. That afternoon I shoot good enough to qualify—along with the rest of the platoon.

4. Breathe. Relax. Aim. Sight. Squeeze.

Years later—forty-eight to be exact—I am visiting a friend in Wyoming who does some competition shooting. He has the civilian version of the M-14 and one afternoon we go out to the rifle range. The gun feels comfortable and familiar, like meeting an old friend you have not seen in years. Muscle memory, I think they call it. I get into a good, stable position and with a good front sight picture fire at a metal moose-shaped target four hundred yards away. There is no wind and I aim a little high to compensate for the bullet drop. Breathe. Relax. Aim. Sight. Squeeeeeze.

My friend looks through a spotting scope. "You hit it," he says, more than a little surprised. "You hit it." I start to explain that I always use the tried-and-true "tit squeezing" marksmanship method ... but decide against it.

"Luck," I say. "Just pure luck."

5

FORTUNATE SON

"I am not afraid of very much. I have been struck by lightning and was in the Marine Corps for four years."—Lee Trevino

Before boot camp I had never heard of Gen. Lewis B. "Chesty" Puller. A legendary Marine general awarded five Navy Crosses in three wars, his outspoken, no-holds-barred demeanor would simply not be tolerated in today's politically correct culture. Once, in the midst of the "Frozen Chosin'" campaign during the Korean War, Chesty gave the order to his Marines to fire on U.S. Army soldiers if they attempted to retreat. Later his son, Lt. Lewis B. Puller Jr., is seriously wounded in Vietnam and loses both legs and a hand. The date of his injury is October 11, 1968. I remember this date because at the time I am on an isolated jungle artillery firebase, a long way from Lt. Puller and in a completely different unit and area, but we still hear about it on the day it happens. Puller was not expected to survive his wounds and at one time got down to just fifty-five pounds. General Puller was devastated, as you might imagine. On seeing his son for the first time in the hospital, Chesty, a steel-hearted warrior and veteran of a hundred battles, broke down sobbing uncontrollably. Lt. Puller said this hurt him far more than any of his wounds.

Lt. Puller wrote a best-selling autobiography about his service and rehabilitation called "Fortunate Son." It is a Pulitzer Prize-winning book titled after the popular Credence Clearwater Revival song. Later, after twenty-five years of struggling with his inner demons, Lt. Puller loses his battle with depression and alcoholism and takes his own life. Another casualty of a war that refuses to end.

Good night, Lt. Puller ... wherever you are.

The drill instructor is looking for a platoon guide—someone to carry the platoon flag and march up front. As leader of the new recruits (even though in reality the guide has absolutely no authority), he is nothing more than a symbol. Kind of like Prince Charles of the royal family. Or perhaps our own vice president.

"All right," the drill instructor says in that raspy sounding voice that is peculiar to all of them, "I want all my struttin' niggers front and center!" This is a little shocking because in the first two weeks of boot camp, in spite of every profane word ever conceived being used prolifically, I never heard the word "nigger." The African American recruits, of which there are quite a few in the platoon, seem to be taken somewhat aback. At least the two I can see directly across the squad bay from my position of attention.

"Don't get your little asses in a tizzy," the drill instructor continues. "Here we call a spade a spade...." In retrospect this episode, like most everything else in boot camp, is apparently done primarily for effect. As inexcusable and bigoted as it seems now, the not-so-subtle message then is: We can say anything we want. We can do anything we want. We have all the power. You have no authority whatsoever and are lower than whale shit at the bottom of the ocean. In fact, you would need to climb a ladder to even get to the whale shit. So, the sooner you accept our absolute and complete control over every facet of your miserable, shitty little lives, the better off you will be.

In fairness, the Marines, generally speaking, are not an overtly racist organization. At least I never saw much evidence of it—other than this one time in boot camp. And I suspect that it was done simply to keep the recruits off balance, intimidated and a little confused. Much later in Vietnam I never hear the "N" word. The fact that everyone is armed to the teeth may have a little something to do with it. But, on reflection, I really don't think so. I think we realized, on a gut level that far outweighs any individually held prejudices, that our lives depend on one another.

Some recruits simply fold as a result of all the screaming, cussing, slapping and constant supervision. Not to mention the seemingly endless lung-burning runs and punishing exercises. It is institutionalized, psychological and oftentimes physical abuse—but with a purpose. The drill instructors are constantly on the prowl for someone beginning to show signs of imploding and zero in on anyone displaying or emitting "non-hacker" signals. Any symptom of mental instability, weakness or rebellion is attacked vigorously. Like coyotes on a wounded rabbit, they show no compassion. The theory is that if you can't take the stress of boot camp,

25

then combat will really push you over the emotional edge. And that is when other Marines die as a result. All true, but still a little disconcerting. Especially if you have had a couple of borderline meltdown moments yourself.

Once, standing at attention in front of my rack I hear a muffled sob. One of the drill instructors, all the way at the other end of the squad bay, apparently hears it too. (They all seem to be remarkably attuned to any slight manifestations of emotional collapse.) The other two drill instructors suddenly appear—from where I don't know, it is like a magic trick—and proceed to turn the crying, hapless recruit into a blubbering, incoherent Looney Tunes basket case. They yell, scream, blow whistles in his ears, place a metal garbage can over his head and beat it with sticks. A couple of Corpsmen eventually lead him away, never to return. The rest of us are standing on line, watching this bizarre incident. Which, I realize now, is all being done for our edification and benefit. As the kid is being loaded into an ambulance, one of the drill instructors yells at him, loud enough for all of us to hear: "Hey, Maggot! I hope your mother and father are on fire right this very minute!"

Later that evening one of the drill instructors gives a class on the proper way to commit suicide with a sharp blade. "Girls," he says holding out his arm, "you slice LONG WAYS. Don't just make a couple of pussy ass scratches across your wrist." (In the mess hall earlier that day a recruit has attempted to slash his wrists with a fork—which our drill instructor says is "pathetic" and ineffective.)

But as the weeks progress we grow stronger, both mentally and physically, in spite of ourselves. The constant exercise and miles' long runs become not exactly easy ... but easier. We march and chant ditties about killing gooks and the symbolic "Jody"—that worthless civilian who is back on the block currently screwing our girlfriends/wives and living the easy civilian life. The drill instructors start to hint, ever so slightly, that maybe, just maybe (so don't get too excited, girls), we may graduate and someday be Marines. Can this be possible? The colorful cursing becomes somewhat ... well, entertaining and downright amusing. As we march along, sounding like a legion of disciplined Roman gladiators, an emotion that can be considered pride slowly begins bubbling to the surface. It is now difficult to keep from laughing at some of the drill instructor's more creative insults. For example, Private Lane (of the vomit mop head), is said to be so dumb he thinks "Moby Dick" is a venereal disease. Some of the Hispanic recruits are said to think "Manual Labor" is a distant cousin.

5. Fortunate Son

At night we are allowed fifteen minutes to shit, shower and shave. The commodes are lined along one wall and the showers are in one small room with four showerheads. If you have bashful kidneys or bowels this can obviously result in problems. The recruits standing "fire watch" duty at night are instructed to not allow more than one recruit at a time in the "head"—a Navy term for bathroom. Furthermore, these nighttime head calls are restricted to three minutes each. Any longer, the drill instructor advises, and the recruit is either sneaking a smoke or seizing an opportunity to "lope his mule." We are generally so exhausted at the end of the day I can't see how this could ever be an issue. If anyone has the energy, after a demanding day on Parris Island, to lope his mule ... well, he has my undying respect and admiration.

There is no privacy and everything must be accomplished at warp speed. One evening we are jammed into the little shower room. One of the drill instructors, who is just passing by, hears someone say something. (There is no talking among ourselves allowed at any time. This is a major, punishable infraction.)

"Well," he says sarcastically, "what do we have here? A garden party? A Chinese clusterfuck? You girls think you can just stand around and shoot the shit in the showers? PUSH-UP POSITION! READY, BEGIN!"

There is standing room only and in the push-up position we are soon a writhing mass of arms and legs. The showers are spraying water and my face is in someone's ass. I have no idea what a Chinese clusterfuck looks like, but this intertwined pile of naked bodies is probably a reasonable facsimile. But this indignity is soon eclipsed by another. Private Lane is next to me and is hung like a bull elephant. In the "down" push-up position his big black donkey dick flops across the top of my hand. Jerking it back in horror, I find much to my dismay that I am unable to do a one-handed push-up.

As unnerving and disgusting as this experience is, there remains one redeeming feature. For the next forty-five years, I have a great and entertaining boot camp story.

6

YOU GUYS HAVE NO IDEA

"Sometimes the heart sees what is invisible to the eye."—H. Jackson Browne

Before being shipped to California and the day after graduation from boot camp, before any leave, we are loaded onto buses headed for Camp Lejeune, North Carolina. Leaving Parris Island counts as one of the happiest days of my life. Little do I know the place will seem like paradise when compared to a variety of successive shitholes in Vietnam. In the Marines everyone is considered and trained to be a basic infantry rifleman. Something about a cook or clerk being able to be pulled from the mess hall or an office and plunked down in a line company. Apparently this occurred a lot in World War II and Korea. I suppose it did happen a time or two in Vietnam—I don't know.

At Lejeune we are assigned to the Infantry Training Regiment, known as ITR. It is a short course in infantry weapons and tactics taught by a sundry collection of war-weary, burned-out Vietnam veteran infantry sergeants and corporals. We do get to fire a lot of neat weapons, though. Bazookas, grenade launchers, and M-60 machine guns. They also have some moving targets, perhaps to simulate some running gooks, and we have a great time blasting away with our big, heavy M-14 rifles. (The M-16s would come later.) And, as a bonus, we get to take some nice long walks in the extensive pine forest that surrounds Camp Lejeune. The food at the battalion mess hall is pure slop. But even with two weeks of mess duty, all in all it is … well, almost enjoyable.

On a twenty-mile march with full packs and rifles through the surrounding woods, a young Marine falls out with heat exhaustion. (I was lying. The long walks were not *that* enjoyable.) Many of the Marines are from northern states and have never experienced the stifling humidity that is common in the American South. At Parris Island the heat is there also, but with some modification. At a certain high temperature a black flag is raised that requires drill instructors to limit excessive physical activity. At the infantry school there are no black flags. Anyway, the kid looks to be in pretty bad shape and the NCOs drench him with water from our canteens in an effort to cool him down. Later, about halfway through the march, we stop for a water break. No water. I have only a few drops left and the guy behind me offers me five dollars for a capful. (Five bucks is a lot of money. We make only eighty-eight dollars a month.) I refuse, as the water suddenly becomes a very precious commodity. I also learn something: When there is nothing available to buy, money has no value. What happened to the heatstroke victim? I am just a little ashamed to say I simply don't remember.

I do remember one incident, though. It sticks in my mind and resurfaces later in Vietnam. A morose and sullen infantry sergeant is instructing a small group of us on searching a prisoner. As in prisoner of war—a POW. Obviously, we were not taking it seriously enough, at least for him. He abruptly stops and gives us a long, silent stare. "You guys have no idea," he says quietly, shaking his head. "Absolutely no fucking idea...."

After my mother passed away some forty-five years later, I find a shoebox she had kept with every letter I had written during my time in the Marines, including the one below. Perhaps I should have realized how difficult this time was for her, as it must be for all families sending off young men to any war. The letters I wrote from Vietnam are all a bunch of fluff with a lot of misinformation about what we were doing. Nothing of any substance. It is hard to write about nothing.

I never told my folks anything but "Don't worry, I am really in a pretty safe place." Sometimes it is true. Most of the time it isn't. Sometimes it is half true.

Farewells are different in times of war. Something, I guess, about the possible finality of the "goodbye." During the Vietnam War there are 58,220 final goodbyes said by departing servicemen. During the Korean War the figure is 54,246. In World War II, 418,500 American military men bid farewell to loved ones for a last time.

My folks take me to the airport in Columbia, South Carolina, and the atmosphere is a little on the melancholy side, but not too bad. Everyone keeps up a pretty good front. That is, until time to board the plane. Then Mom grabs me with a surprisingly strong grip, sobbing, and refuses to let go. She creates quite a little scene, which for her is totally out of character. Dad pries her hands loose so I can board the plane.

Once I get seated, a sailor sitting next to me wants to engage in a little social chitchat. I don't feel like talking. In fact, I kind of feel more like crying.

Dear Mom and Dad:

Well, here I am at Camp Pendleton after that too short ten-day boot-camp leave. I am just not that impressed with Southern California. I think California is playing a joke on the rest of the country. It ain't that nice. At least the part I have seen.

Schoolteacher June Jones, 1945, in Fonde, Kentucky.

I am now in what they call a Casual Company, although things are not casual enough for me, waiting for an artillery school to start. They are going to attempt to make me a Fire Control Man. Whatever that is. Something to do with artillery. It doesn't sound like it will be too bad. We shall see soon enough.

The last couple of days I have been assigned to pick up trash along the roadways with a bunch of prisoners from the brig. (No, I am not in jail—yet!) I have a stick with a nail in the end and kind of walk around on my own. Could be a lot worse. At noon chow, I go to the mess hall. At the end of the day, I go back to the barracks, and everyone else (the jailbirds) go back to the brig. It is kind of interesting to see folk's reaction as they pass me in their cars. I know they are probably thinking, "I wonder what this loser did?" When I smile pleasantly and wave, they always look away.

Last weekend me and a couple of guys from boot camp went to Disneyland. It was entertaining and we saw a lot of "Goofy" characters. This is before we even GOT to Disneyland. California is a strange place with even stranger people. The Land of Fruits and Nuts. A lot of families with kids were at Disneyland. Which seems kind of weird to me as everybody I know is getting ready to go to war. Forgot there are still kids and folks around leading normal lives ... taking vacations, etc. That is the American way, I guess. To heck with Vietnam, let's all go to Disneyland!

Anyway, here is my best guess as to what will happen over the next couple of months. As near as I can figure out anyway. (The Marines keep you in the dark and never tell you anything.) After this artillery school, the next thing is something they call "staging." It is some kind of training to get you ready for Vietnam. I don't think it has anything to do with a stage. (The next one leaves in ten minutes. I would like to be on it.) That is when they issue the new rifles you have been seeing on the news called M-16's. I have been reading and hearing about them. Never seen one except on T.V. (I hope mine works.) Also, we get a bunch of shots before flying off to Okinawa. The Marines call it "Okie." A couple weeks there and then off to the Tropical Paradise! I am hoping this thing won't last another 13 months and everybody can come home. Doesn't hurt to think positive.

Sorry to hear brother David is going to register with Selective Service. I didn't realize he was that close to being 18. Maybe he should burn his draft card. Just kidding! (I think.) Hope he is taking good care of my car. [Once I got to Vietnam and was there for a while, my brother, twenty-five years later, told me I wrote him a letter and said, "Whatever you have to do ... don't come over here." I don't remember writing it, but have no doubt this is true. Later he did receive a pre-induction notice while I was in Vietnam. My dad went down to the draft board. My brother was not drafted and Dad never revealed what he said or did...]

Don't have a mailing address yet. Will call you when I get one so you can keep those cards and letters pouring in! Today me and a couple of other "losers" have been assigned to wax the barracks. The sergeant is gone so we have not done anything so far but pretend to work and lie around listening to Wolfman Jack on the radio. Got to go. The sergeant just pulled up.

Love, Bill

7

SHREDDED WHEAT

"The twenty-four percent unemployment reached at the depth of the Great Depression was no picnic."—Barry Eichengreen

At Camp Pendleton, California, a flight to Okinawa, the first stop en route to South Vietnam, is scheduled ... one week away. Apprehension is high and several Marines do not return from weekend liberty in nearby Oceanside. (Also called Oceanslime...) A permanent party administration sergeant has recently spread the word that he needs a clerk who will be reassigned and remain stateside. Any takers? The cost is five hundred dollars. It is a bribe, pure and simple. At this time the base pay for a private first class is around one hundred ten a month.

I call my dad on a payphone and let him know of this new "opportunity." There is a long silence on his end. "Well," he finally says, "you do whatever you think best. I will support you no matter what your choice. And if you need five hundred dollars, I will send it to you...." At the time, because of his nonjudgmental response, I feel more affection for my dad than probably any other time I can remember. His reaction surprises me, but more or less seals my fate. Now there is no way I can opt out and spend the war as a Remington Raider in some stifling administration office in Southern California. Plus, I am somewhat enamored with the adventure of going off to war, and returning in glory a hero to bask in the adoring glory and admiration of friends, family and beautiful women. (Decades later, the sheer foolishness of this fantasy is difficult to comprehend.)

After the Japanese attack Pearl Harbor, Dad quits high school and joins the Army Air Corps. At least that was my impression for fifty years. Just prior to his death I ask him why he chose to get into the "flying part" of the military. Did you always like airplanes? Did Lindberg's historic cross-Atlantic flight create a fascination with airplanes and flying? A little irritated, he says: "I didn't join the Army Air Corps. I didn't join anything but the Army. That is where they sent me."

The shadow of the Great Depression never leaves him. One of his first childhood memories is scrounging through the Knoxville, Tennessee, city dump as he and his father search for edible produce and other food items. Once, they discover a large amount of moldy shredded wheat—a virtual bonanza. They scrape off the green stuff, and, for weeks, eat it anyway. Till the day he is admitted to the nursing home, some sixty-five years later, he never permits shredded wheat in his home.

Caldwell Jones, U.S. Army Air Corps, 1943.

One family story reaches near-mythical proportions. My paternal grandfather is dying of pneumonia in the charity ward of a Knoxville hospital. The medical staff has already "pulled the curtain," which is symbolic of imminent death. My grandmother, with my then four-year-old dad and his six-year-old sister, is at the end of her emotional rope. Rather than watch her two children slowly starve, her pathetic and desperate plan, on my grandfather's death, is to mercifully kill her two children and then herself...

A bootlegger uncle, estranged from the family and somewhat of a black sheep, arrives at the hospital unannounced and gives my grandmother a fifty dollar bill. In 1929, this is a small fortune. That same night, a coal-miner friend of my grandfather comes to visit with a bottle of whiskey and some rock candy. He spoon-feeds my ailing grandfather throughout the night. The next morning there seems to be some improvement. In a week, miraculously, he goes home.

The Army Air Corps sends Dad to gunnery school and apparently he does well. Always an excellent shot, he is made an instructor and sent to Florida to train aircraft gunners for the 8th Air Force's monumental air war over the skies of Europe. The assignment inadvertently becomes one of the great tragedies of his life. Sending crews he trained overseas, later to hear they are shot down over the flak-filled skies of France and Germany, results in "survivor's guilt" that plagues him till the day he dies. He pleads to be sent into combat, even at one point seeking a transfer to the infantry. The squadron commander (who Dad says looks like Wallace Beery) explains there is important and valuable work to be done on the home front. There will be no transfers. Later, I learn that training is almost as dangerous as actual combat. The Army Air Corps loses over 25,000 men in training accidents before we drop the first bomb on Nazi Germany.

Of all Dad's stories, one in particular stands out. Toward the end of World War II, the Air Corps is recycling air crews back into combat which, for some reason or another, do not complete their required missions. A gunner, who had previously bailed out of a crippled bomber, is being re-qualified before being sent back. He does not want to go. During his combat tour, while on a low-level strafing mission over Germany, he machine-guns an old woman and a child running down some railroad tracks. ("This would be easy to do," Dad says. "Going almost three-hundred miles an hour and shooting everything that moves ... it is an understandable mistake.") This unfortunate and tragic event haunts the gunner and he yells and screams in his sleep and bails out of the top bunk. Dad tells the story in isolated pieces to me over 50 years. Never all at once.

"The cadre at the gunnery school suspects this guy is failing all the tests on purpose," Dad says, "so he will not have to go back." The traumatized gunner reminds me somewhat of my shit-burning private in Vietnam. Both warriors, though years apart, have reached their psychological Mount Everest and simply refuse to participate any longer. "Anyway," Dad continues, "everyone knows he is flunking out on purpose. Nobody can be that bad of a shot. So we pass him."

Around 1952 Dad is back in what is now called the U.S. Air Force. (He always said he likes the Army better as, in his words, the Air Force tends to be "chickenshit." My mother and brother ride a train from Kentucky to Luke Air Force Base in Phoenix, Arizona. Dad buys a little cinder-block yellow house in a newly developed neighborhood. Like many new homeowners, he quickly learns there is more expense to home ownership than merely making the mortgage payments. At the time, he is a crewmember on a medium-size bomber pulling targets for fighter jets headed to the air war over Korea. Out at four a.m., he flies the first mission of the day and gets a job delivering telegrams for Western Union in the afternoons and evenings. Even with flight pay, which is half of base pay, there isn't enough money to go around.

One afternoon he comes by the house to pick me up as he is working his telegram job. Driving an old 1939 Chevrolet named "Jezebel" (I later learn he picked the name Jezebel because she is generally an unreliable and cantankerous wench), he asks me if I want to go to the circus. What a question! Name any five-year-old kid who doesn't want to go to the circus. In reality, we cannot afford to go to the circus, but Dad is simply delivering a telegram to one of the performers. Clyde Beatty, a world-famous wild animal trainer, is the intended recipient.

Standing next to Dad in the front of Jezebel (no car seats or seat belts in those days) we head to the Big Top. A circus worker directs us to Clyde Beatty's travel trailer on the back lot. Elephants, tigers in cages, a lot of strange sights and smells. Dad takes the telegram up to the front door as I wait in Jezebel. Clyde comes to the door wearing a wife beater T-shirt and with shaving cream all over his face. Dad hands him the telegram and hurries back to the car.

"Did you see him?" he asks excitedly. "Did you see Clyde Beatty?"

This is way better than any chickenshit circus. Clyde Beatty in the flesh. Shaving. Of course I saw him. In fact, I can still see him now...

A couple of years later Dad is transferred to Florida and then to Tripoli, Libya. We follow him like an itinerant troop of gypsies, another brother now on the scene. In Tripoli we live in a downtown villa surrounded by concrete walls with tops lined with broken glass. The local Arabs steal anything not nailed down and even break in our house as we sleep inside. Eventually we hire a guard who sleeps in our garage and walks around with a big wooden club. We are in the middle of Ali Baba and his forty thieves. Trying to play with the local Arab kids, they steal my toys and footballs. Once, furious at their blatant thievery, I retrieve my BB gun and fire away as they run in all directions. I almost put a young Arab boy's eye out in the process. Not my finest hour. My mom, in her naiveté, will sometimes attempt to share her Christian faith with the locals who speak English. This works out about like you might expect. Just imagine, if you will, a Muslim attempting to convert a delegate to the Southern Baptist Convention. I remember one young Arab man saying: "Jesus good, good man. Just like Mohammed!" As Americans, somewhat arrogant and feeling smugly superior, we have immersed ourselves in a culture we do not understand and with a language we do not speak. Sound familiar? Perhaps our prejudices are all hardwired and we will never learn. Everyone does not think like us nor do they all want to be Americans. Shocking...

After a year or so in town we move onto Wheelus Air Force Base and into base housing. With few exceptions, Arabs are not allowed on the military installation. It is Little America with bowling alleys, ice cream shops, and dependent schools. I join a Little League baseball team in a vain attempt to improve my nonexistent athletic skills. One afternoon after school we show up for practice. Our coach never arrives and back home I learn that he—a pilot—crashed that day and is lost at sea. This is the first person I know personally who dies and it seems strange and surreal. Batting practice one day; gone forever the next. Sixty years later the count is now ... well, more than I want to remember.

Dad is still pulling targets but now is a back seater in a twin-engine jet bomber—a B-57 Canberra painted bright orange to prevent hotshot fighter pilots from shooting it down by mistake. I suppose it is dangerous, at least one of the airmen who works for him is killed. One of the young guys in his unit mentions it in my presence but a look from Dad silences him immediately. I never find out the details.

One incident during this North African tour sticks in my memory. My dad takes a thirty-day leave and the family hops a military flight to Rome, Italy, on a vacation to tour Europe. The aircraft is an old C-47 with bucket seats and parachutes. The same type of plane that dropped twenty thousand or so paratroopers over France during the D-day invasion. Maybe even one of the same airplanes—it isn't that long after the end of World War II. At age ten my imagination works overtime. For a few moments, I *am* a paratrooper with the 101st Airborne, June 6, 1944. Stand up! Hook up! Stand in the door! My fantasy is interrupted when one of the pilots comes back into the cabin and asks my dad if he wants to fly the plane for a while. This surprises me as Dad is not a qualified Air Force pilot, nor is he an officer. This is akin to an American Airlines pilot coming back and offering one of the paying passengers a chance to fly the plane. Dad jumps at the chance and heads for the cockpit. An hour or so later he comes swaggering back to the cabin smirking like a tomcat that just ate a cage full of prized parakeets. "Notice," he confides to me, "how smooth the flight was when I was at the controls." All this macho posturing, I realize now, is done solely for my benefit.

7. *Shredded Wheat*

Perhaps a disclaimer is in order relative to the previous little vignette. Dad does in fact do a lot of flying from the back seat of the bomber. The pilot of the C-47 obviously knows him. And between wars, while a civilian, Dad *did* obtain a commercial pilot's license. Nevertheless, the incident impresses the shit out of a fourth grader.

No perfect father has ever existed, and Dad was certainly not perfect. But I also was far, far from a perfect son. So I guess that evens things out. Between wars, Dad plays some professional softball, and although he never says anything, I can always tell he is a little disappointed in my lack of athletic ability. As we both age and mature, we grow closer. More like old friends than father and son. Our roles reverse in the later years and my mother will threaten to "rat him out" to me when he becomes uncooperative with doctor's orders and medicine routines. Somewhat grudgingly, he always pays his taxes. (He paid a lot of taxes!) Loyal to his family, church and country, he keeps the same two business partners for almost forty-five years. Even stumbling through the fog of Alzheimer's, he never gives up. At his funeral, two former employees, both of whom Dad fired years ago, show up for the services. Not a bad legacy. Not bad at all.

The last year of his life is spent in the best nursing home we can find, but I am unsure if there is such a thing as a "good nursing home." They are simply waiting rooms. Increasingly confused, Dad sometimes thinks he runs the entire facility. Escaping twice, his plans are often discovered because he tends to share details with the nursing home staff. ("I thought the maintenance man was my friend. He is not to be trusted....") Always a gentleman, he is a favorite of all the employees.

In his last days, Dad cannot remember if he has eaten breakfast. No short-term memory to speak of ... hardly any. Sometimes he confuses me with my younger brother. But he remembers the events of World War II with striking clarity, so we often talk of those days in particular.

"Dad," I ask him one afternoon, "remember the story of the guy who keeps flunking the training exercise? The one who would bail out of his bunk?"

There is a look of recognition. "Sure," he replies. "Of course I remember."

"Well, whatever happened to him? All these years you never said what happened to him." Dad's expression changes. Perhaps I should have left this alone.

Dad gazes in silence for a minute or two out into the nursing home courtyard. "He never did have to go back," he finally says. "He killed himself." There is a pause before he speaks again.

"And," he says quietly, "he was not the only one..."

A week later, his family all around him, Dad takes a couple of labored breaths and then slips away.

8

A LIVE DOG ...
A DEAD LION

*"Take this job and shove it, I ain't working here no more."—Johnny Pay-
check*

Third Battalion, 12th Marines, 3rd Marine Division Headquarters.
September 1968. It is not the worst place one could choose to spend a
war. The battalion headquarters at Quang Tri, South Vietnam, has a mess
hall where the chow is semi-edible. Barracks are plywood—"hooches" with
some nearby cold-water showers. At the enlisted men's club, a world-class
sound system pounds out Janis Joplin and Jimi Hendrix. While listening
to Procol Harum wail "A Whiter Shade of Pale," it is sometimes possible
to forget you are even in Vietnam. The fifteen-cent beer also helps quite
a bit. In the rear with the gear and the beer. All in all, not a bad life.

The proverbial fly in this otherwise somewhat pleasant mix is my job.
As a new guy, or FNG (an acronym that is easy to decipher), my assignment is to burn the shitters. Human waste does not burn easily. It is necessary to pull 55 gallon drums, cut in half and placed strategically beneath
a "three holer," douse the contents with diesel fuel, and set the unholy
mess ablaze.

The top layer burns easily enough, but what remains must be stirred
like soup in a giant cauldron. The smoke and noxious smells are ines-
capable, saturating clothes and hair and clinging to the back of your
throat. To say this task is unpleasant is perhaps the mother of all euphe-
misms.

A story making the rounds, no doubt on the same level as an urban
myth, relates how a newly arrived FNG is assigned to this particular detail.
Unfortunately, someone fails in his responsibility to issue proper instructions. An inferno at the officer's facility ensues. Rather than pull the barrels

out, he sets the whole building on fire. As flames leap skyward, he patiently explains that his orders were to "burn the shitters."

After about a week, a young private shows up one morning to be my "assistant." Since I am a private first class, I take this as an opportunity to showcase my leadership potential. Apparently this whole assignment, shitty as it is, is merely a test the Marines have orchestrated to determine my suitability for much bigger and better responsibilities. I resolve to become the most efficient shit-burning private first class in the history of the Marine Corps.

As fate would have it, though, my new charge knows considerably more about burning shit than I do. He is not an FNG, and this assignment is not his first shit-burning rodeo. In country for over six months, he initially is sent to an artillery battery on the DMZ. Wounded twice (though by his own admission not seriously), he decides he has had enough.

"I am not going back," he informs the first sergeant. "Do whatever you want with me." Incidentally, this seems an act of bravery in and of itself. The first sergeant is a thirty-year man who picks his teeth with a nail. He looks like a weight-lifting bulldog with a crew cut.

My assistant, a young kid not long out of high school from somewhere in the Midwest, explains his reasoning to me thusly: "They are trying to kill me," he says. "Two chances is all they get...."

"Who is trying to kill you?" I ask. He looks at me like I have a foot-long penis growing out of my ear. Maybe even both ears.

"The gooks!" he replies. "Who do you think? The gooks!"

Strangely enough, this pronouncement is a revelation. Even after boot camp, infantry and artillery school, the idea that "gooks" are trying to kill us is still surprising. By "us" I mean Marines and by extension ... me. This rear-area shit-burning job is looking better all the time.

At the mess hall, my assistant and I have a table all to ourselves, no doubt having something to do with our present occupation. We talk. My private has been busted and threatened with the brig. Even his present job is an attempt to shame him into submission. Nothing works. An appointment with a military shrink does not go well, especially after he tells the psychiatrist officer that "if he felt that strongly about returning to duty, maybe he should get his own fat ass up on the DMZ."

It seems somewhat of a stretch to call someone twice wounded a coward, but apparently those in positions of safety have no qualms in doing so. Suspected cowardice is embarrassing to those in no danger. Later

40

I find those in actual combat are far more reluctant to pass judgment. Everyone, they would usually say, has a breaking point.

One morning we are halfheartedly going about our duties when my reluctant warrior splashes some diesel fuel on his legs. Too close to the flames, his clothes catch on fire. As he rolls on the ground, we extinguish his smoldering trousers by beating them with our hands. One leg is already starting to blister. It is not a minor burn.

As he hobbles toward the Battalion Aid Station, a bit of Scripture comes to mind. "A live dog is better than a dead lion." But this is not really accurate. The kid is not a dog or a lion, just a skinny eighteen-year-old who has seen war up close and finally decides he has had enough. It briefly occurs to me that I have never seen him smile.

I never see him again.

9

A WORLD OF SHIT

"You will kill ten of us, we will kill one of you, but in the end, you will tire of it first."—Ho Chi Minh

At the morning formation, 1st Sgt. Bulldog stands before us with his ever present clipboard. We are a motley collection of FNGs, office pinkies, cooks, and Marines going on or returning from R&R, which means rest and recreation. I later learn that everyone gets a week or so in a Southeast Asia fleshpot, usually toward the end of their thirteen-month tour. The troops have appropriately renamed this practice A&A, which stands for ass and alcohol.

Bulldog glances at me and looks down at his clipboard roster. I have not been in country long enough for him to even know my name. Which is not necessarily a bad thing.

"Jones," he growls, "go to supply and draw some warfighting gear. The convoy leaves at oh eight hundred. You are going north." He notices my look of bewilderment and this seems to amuse him. There is a hint of a smile. "Surely," he says, "you didn't expect to stay here burning shit for the next year?"

I am unsure if he expects a response so I don't answer, but the truth is I would be very content to stay right here for the next twelve months. Besides, I have streamlined this whole shit-burning process and can get it done in about four hours. The rest of the day is mine. ("What did you do in the war, Daddy?" "Well, it was really pretty bad. I don't want to talk about it. Just say I was in a world of shit....")

An hour later I am in the back of a large open-back truck with a fifty-caliber machine gun mounted over the cab. A black Marine, wearing a flak jacket and sporting a red bandanna around his neck, is loading the gun and caressing it like his old girlfriend back on the block. "We got into an ambush last week," he says, patting the big gun affectionately, "and she done real good...." None of this helps to reduce my anxiety level.

Before we leave, Bulldog shows up with a red nylon mailbag and a case of Cokes. "When you get to VCB [Vandergrift Combat Base], go to the LZ and wait for a chopper. When one comes in going to Fire Support Base Alpine, get your ass on it. Take this mail and these Cokes. They know you are coming." This, at least, is somewhat reassuring. He turns to leave but has an afterthought. Again, there is a tiny hint of a smile. "One more thing," he barks. "Good luck."

Struggling aboard with my weapon, gear, mailbag and Cokes, I notice one Marine kind of taking charge. The other Marines on board treat him with a kind of deference. I think he may be an officer. But he sure doesn't look like a typical officer. No insignia and he has a large handlebar mustache. A lock of hair, Hitler style, sweeps down rakishly over one eye. Obviously I don't know what is going on and he turns his attention to me.

"You!" he says, not unkindly. "Sit over here next to me."

As a lost dog in an unfamiliar neighborhood, I am thankful someone is telling me what to do. "Yes, Sir!" I reply, maybe a little too eagerly.

"Don't call me Sir," he says. "I work for a living. I am not nor will I ever be a Sir. Call me Hutch. That is my name."

I then notice he has a sergeant's chevron on one collar. Later, I learn he is on his third tour and is an artillery forward observer. Somewhat of a local Marine legend, he is a man who has found his life's calling in Vietnam. A fearless and competent free spirit who even the officers and staff NCO's treat with respect and often ask for advice. He is also crazy as hell.

We sit facing outboard on both sides of the truck with rifles at the ready. Ready for what? I don't have the first clue or slightest indication, having only been in Vietnam a couple of weeks. "If anything at all happens on this trip," Hutch instructs, "watch me and do EXACTLY everything I do." Which is precisely what I was planning to do anyway. If Hutch even scratches his balls, I will immediately follow suit and scratch mine, as this may very well be some sort of important superstitious act.

In the 1950s, the French named Highway One "The Street Without Joy." Proceeding north on what is a red clay dirt road, we roll past rice paddies and sad little villages. Black pajama-clad women, with matching black teeth, and old men with stringy long beards either stare blankly at us or ignore us completely. Perhaps, I think, they do not realize we are here to save them from the evils of Communism. Kids from two to ten

43

years old stretch out their hands hoping we will throw them something. Candy, cigarettes, C-rations. Anything. The road has been named accurately by the French. I am not feeling much, if any, joy. At Dong Ha the little convoy turns west on Route 9 toward Vandergrift Combat Base.

Rolling toward the mountains that are the typical of Quang Tri Province, it is difficult to ignore the beauty of the country. The lush, varied shades of tropical green are awe inspiring and beautiful. The other Marines on board are quiet and alert, displaying an air of confident nonchalance. They are a ragged collection of veterans who have seen it all already. As an FNG, with the exception of Hutch, they completely ignore me. I am curiously envious of their status and attitude.

Someday, though, if I can stay alive long enough, I hope to be just like them.

10

CHICKEN PLATES

"I thought: ya know,
If I ever write a book,
I should remember
This moment."
    —Rod McQueary

The convoy reaches Vandegrift Combat Base after several hours and my mentor and protector, Sergeant Hutch, disappears. It seems Hutch's status allows him to come and go as he pleases. Apparently he rotates between grunt and artillery units, showing up where he feels the "hunting" will be the best. At least that is how it appears to me.

Vandegrift is a large supply base/firebase that used to be known as LZ Stud. It is surrounded by mountains in a little valley that provides an excellent tactical advantage for the North Vietnamese Army to mortar and rocket, which it does, on a fairly regular basis. The name LZ Stud offended someone's sensibilities and has been renamed Vandegrift for a Marine general and Medal of Honor winner. Most of the Marines, at least the older veterans, still call it LZ Stud. It's a little more macho, and Marines have a tendency to overdose on the whole "macho" thing.

Helicopters are constantly coming and going from the little landing zone in the middle of the base. A Marine, radio strapped to his back, pops yellow and purple smoke grenades and directs the big twin-rotor choppers down as they blow red clay dust, rainbow-colored smoke, and anything not nailed down in all directions. He yells out destinations, usually an artillery firebase or a unit name, as groups from a couple hundred waiting Marines "saddle up" and shuffle aboard. With my red nylon mailbag and case of Cokes, I wait, somewhat impatiently, for the magic words—"LZ Alpine." It doesn't come until the next morning.

It is my first ride in a helicopter. There will be many, many more. The

45

Landing zone at Vandergrift Combat Base, October 1968.

noise is a surprise and the seats are not airline quality, if you could even call them seats. Two Marines in flight suits and helmets man machine guns at windows on both sides of the chopper. With their helmet visors down and pistols worn gunslinger style, they look up to the task at hand. More of that macho thing. In addition, there are steel plates strapped to their chests called "chicken plates." Why they are so named is a mystery. To me there is nothing "chicken" about not wanting to be shot through the heart. Chalk it up to the warped sense of black humor prevalent among combat troops everywhere.

It is difficult to hear with the rotor whine and engine noise, but nobody is talking anyway. Smells of jet fuel and hydraulic fluid fill the cabin. The other Marines are taking this opportunity to doze, in the manner of sleep-deprived infantry in any war zone. The blond-headed kid next to me has horn-rimmed glasses and is as relaxed as if he were riding a school bus home. Which probably wasn't that long ago. He looks considerably younger than me. Above the roar he asks me pleasantly, "First time?" I am so new that I might as well be, like Minnie Pearl, wearing a price tag. Nodding my head yes, he counters with "Come on, I'll show you around."

10. Chicken Plates

Show me around? What is he, the local tour guide? Just a private first class and passenger (like me), he heads toward the cockpit in front of the aircraft. For some unknown reason I follow him. We stand behind the two pilots and watch them for a few minutes. Neither pays any more attention to us than if we had been two buzzing houseflies. The two gunners are equally oblivious. Bored and disinterested, they lean over their guns staring into the flowing green jungle beneath us. It is like we are invisible.

Motioning for me to follow him, my school bus companion goes to the rear of the chopper. We crawl up on the ramp and peer over the side and my new best friend points out areas of interest. The Rock Pile. Route Nine. A lot of jungle pockmarked with water-filled bomb craters. Not long out of boot camp, where you are told when and where to eat, sleep and pee, I am sure we are not allowed to do this and will be in some sort of trouble. My tour director senses my apprehension and grins knowingly.

Back in our "seats," we fly toward Fire Support Base Alpine and our collective fates ... wherever and whatever that is. My new friend then gives me some parting words of advice: "This is Vietnam," he yells into my ear. "Just remember, nobody gives a fuck." Years later, that statement still holds a timeless truth.

One of the waste gunners holds up two fingers. We are getting ready to land and "unass" the chopper and everyone begins to adjust their gear. We descend rapidly and the ramp comes down. I begin to leisurely gather my pack, weapon, Cokes and mailbag like I was on a Delta flight landing in Atlanta. But looking around, I am the only one still here. The two gunners, who earlier I thought might even be asleep at their guns, have spontaneously combusted into screaming, insane devils. They are pushing and yelling and throwing off my mailbag and Cokes even as the chopper is lifting off.

Later I learn that on these outlying firebases, the choppers don't like to stay on the ground more than five or ten seconds. Any longer and it invites a rainstorm of mortars. Apparently the gooks get some sort of special medal for shooting down an American helicopter. It doesn't take much. Knock off a couple rotor blades and time in the air is severely compromised. During the Vietnam War, over five thousand helicopters either crashed or got shot from the sky. So you can't really blame the gunners. You are not paranoid if someone really *is* out to kill you.

As the chopper wops away into the distance, I am standing alone on the little LZ. The mailbag and Cokes have vanished. Someone has already picked them up. To the northwest, Tiger Tooth Mountain, known for its shape, looms menacingly. To the north are more mountains. The hill has two batteries of artillery and is surrounded by jungle. There are no signs of civilization in sight. Living conditions look primitive. The Marines are living in holes and I think fondly of my shit-burning job in the rear.

A skinny, shirtless Marine walks fast toward me. He is grinning like a demented mule eating briars. "Thank God you're here," he says. "You are my replacement."

11

MAGNIFICENT BASTARDS

"Above all, Vietnam was a war that asked everything of a few Americans and nothing of most in America."—Myra MacPherson

The one-man welcoming committee at Fire Support Alpine is a little too glad to see me for my taste. I follow him to a bunker where he says I am assigned. It is the Fire Direction Center of an artillery battery of 105 millimeter howitzer cannons. Two hissing Coleman lanterns provide light. A couple of radios squeal and a gunnery sergeant supervises six Marines engaged in a variety of activities. There is a distinct smell of body odor, to which I soon grow accustomed and also contribute.

The gunnery sergeant (Gunny) is a small pale-faced man who seldom sees the light of day. At one time I think perhaps he more or less lives in the bunker, because it is safer there than being outside. Much later, I learn this not to be true. He is a pleasant man who will, if necessary, expose himself to fire and danger to get the job done. Friendly and talkative, Gunny keeps the atmosphere relaxed and efficient. Mistakes in the FDC are deadly and other Marines, grunts mostly, die as a result of errors made here. I will spend most of the next year in a bunker somewhere similar to this one calculating ranges, deflections and powder charges for the big guns. Killing gooks with a pencil...

Gunny introduces me around. Perhaps remembering their own first days as an FNG, the guys are reasonably amiable. One Marine named Andrews sits before a large map and is apparently the unit's self-appointed morale booster. To the amusement of the others, he keeps up a constant patter of wiseass comments and entertaining bullshit. Later transferred, I hear through the lance corporal grapevine that he is wounded and sent home with no legs. (I never follow up on it, hoping it is a rumor and not wanting to know the truth.)

49

Artillery is devastating and causes over eighty-five percent of casualties in any war. "With teamwork," Gunny says, "we can put a round in a gook's back pocket from seven miles away. It is a beautiful thing." A 155 millimeter cannon has a range of eleven miles or so—a little further than our 105 millimeter cannons. The bigger guns, mostly the Army's 175 millimeter "Long Toms," can reach a target up to twenty-five miles away. A battery of howitzers, usually six, firing on a single target must seem like the end of the world to those on the receiving end. For many it is.

The words "fire mission" are heard on the radio. A forward observer, miles away, gives map coordinates and the Marines get busy sticking pins in maps and measuring distances. Andrews is in the middle of some long story with no apparent point and Gunny tells him to "shut the fuck up." (But he smiles as he says it.) The information, called "dope," is transmitted to the gun crews via a sound-powered headset and soon a white phosphorous "spotter" round is on the way. The artillery forward observer (FO), who is the eyes of the artillery, then makes an adjustment and calls "fire for effect." In minutes, eighteen rounds of high-explosive shells pulverize a piece of Vietnam jungle real estate the size of a football field into garden mulch. If any people are there, they are mulch now, too.

The two batteries on LZ Alpine are in support of the Fourth Marines, an infantry regiment known as "the Magnificent Bastards." The artillery is known as "the Long Arm of the Magnificent Bastards." Although

"FNG." Author at two months in-country.

50

we are not grunts (infantry), we still live like dogs on these firebases. The grunts, however, live worse than dogs. Plus, they "hump" the jungle hills with enough gear to cripple a good packhorse. On these outlying firebases, trouble usually comes to us. The grunts go out looking for it. They may or may not be bastards.

But they are most certainly courageous and magnificent.

12

A MEXICAN ANGEL

"All the wrong people remember Vietnam. I think all the people who remember it should forget it. And all the people who forgot it should remember it."—Michael Herr

Gunny sends someone with me on that first day to "find a hole." We go to the side of the hill and find a small bunker big enough for one man. My new home is a red clay cave with sandbags stacked strategically around it. "Get something to eat," he says, "and I will be back for you later. Gunny wants you to spend some time in the FDC just watching for a couple days."

Cannons boom sporadically. A large helicopter is dropping off a pallet of ammo on the LZ. There is the all-too-familiar smell of burning shit from the two barrels on top of the hill. Three weeks in country with twelve months and one week to go. A sinking feeling, accompanied by a knot in the pit of my stomach, begins to form. One day at a time, I tell myself. One day at a time...

A can of C-ration fruit cocktail helps keep the feeling at bay. But not much. With the fruit-cocktail can empty, I fill it with water and attempt to make coffee. A heat tablet fills the small cave with nose-burning, eye-watering fumes. By this time I am not floundering in self-pity; I am *drowning* in it. Despite my best efforts, I start sinking into a swirling whirlpool of despair.

I send up a little prayer. Although at age twenty I have never done much praying, I surmise it sure couldn't hurt. With no other options, it seems like the prudent thing to do. A few moments later, much to my astonishment, an angel shows up at the entrance to my little one-man bunker.

Well ... maybe not your typical white-robed, winged angel. This angel is a chubby Mexican kid named Randy Ortega from Dallas, Texas. He's from a gun crew on the other side of the hill, and I have no idea what he is doing here. Inviting himself in, he takes charge of my coffee-making project. "The first thing you need to do," the angel says, "is throw away these fucking heat tablets." He retrieves a block of C-4 plastic explosive from a pants pocket. It is the consistency of modeling clay, and he rolls a little piece into a ball. A makeshift stove, fashioned from an empty C-ration can, is produced from another pocket. He lights the C-4 in the little stove and places the can of water on top. In four seconds we have boiling water.

Ortega talks nonstop, punctuating his commentary with drill instructor marching cadence sounds. When he returns home, he plans to go to work for Neiman-Marcus Department Store, where, he says, "rich people buy shit." In spite of myself, I am smiling at his bubbling friendliness and outrageous stream of bullshit. He opens his flak jacket and displays a hole about the size of a quarter on the edge of it. "Shrapnel," he explains. "Gooks mortared us a couple days ago...." He leans forward as if to tell me an intimate little secret. "But they will never, never get me," he confides slyly. "Why? Because I am way, way too fast for the little gook bastards. Little do they know that I AM [interjecting some bullfighting trumpet sounds here] SUPERMEX!" He does a little Mexican Hat Dance step, gives me half a block of C-4, and is gone. I hear a drill instructor growling cadence in the distance as he walks away.

Sipping coffee that is bordering too hot, I contemplate the encounter with this angel disguised as a likable and entertaining Mexican kid. From near clinical depression fifteen minutes ago, my spirits are now soaring. Maybe, with the help of some of these crazy-ass Marines, I *can* get through this thing after all.

FIXATION

The fiery crash growls
Low and evil sounds
Rattle the earth
A fighter plane
Follows tracer round
Into a red hillside.

Later, a pilot tells what happens
"You get tunnel vision," he says
"Become obsessed with the target
Forget to pull up."
We sit silent
In sandbagged reflection
Chavez makes the sign of the cross
"At least," he says
"He has on dry sox."

It is an omen
Dark and subtle
Of our own Nam madness
Mission successful—target destroyed
But in the end
We kill ourselves.

13

You Will Probably Get Killed Anyway

"My way of joking is to tell the truth. That is the funniest joke in the world."—Mohammed Ali

In a dark, damp bunker candle light flickers as we listen to sixties music on a battery-powered cassette player. One of the Marines lights a joint and wordlessly passes it around. Never having even smelled marijuana before, much less having smoked any, I decline and pass the fat little cigarette to the man on my left. This is the drug-crazed sixties and the dope culture is alive and well within America's military. It is infinitely worse in the rear areas, but combat troops also have their share of "heads." If the officers know about the drug use, they choose to do little about it.

These Marines do not know me that well, but they seem unconcerned about smoking dope in my presence. Perhaps, I think, the element of trust is such that they know even an FNG will keep silent. But there is a more plausible reason ... they don't care. Living in holes with rats, the Marines rationalize that any punishment, if caught, will be an improvement. The standard question when contemplating consequences is: "What are they going to do? Send me to Vietnam?"

Actually, drug use among Marine line units is not as prevalent as with rear echelon troops. First, because nobody wants to stand lines with someone stoned. Also, in the "bush" for weeks and sometimes months at a time, there is no possibility of purchasing any dope. Nobody here but rats, monkeys, tigers, big snakes, the North Vietnamese Army, and us.

After passing the joint, the kid next to me confides that he never smoked any dope before he got to "this fucking place. But, over here, what the hell...." He shrugs and smiles, adding, "You'll probably get killed anyway." This cavalier sense of fatalism is common in the Green Machine and

57

is strangely part of its tradition, pride and mystery. It is also, in some ways, part of its magic and power. It starts in boot camp when individual pictures are taken. "Don't smile, girls," the drill instructor orders. "This is going to be your killed-in-action photo."

The next time the joint comes around I inhale a big lung full and hold it in like I see the others do. It doesn't seem to have much effect. But the conversation, which previously was mildly amusing, now becomes the funniest thing I have ever heard. A song, "MacArthur's Park," is playing on the cassette recorder. Some of the lyrics include: "Someone left a cake out in the rain/I don't think that I can take it/Cause it took so long to bake it/And I'll never have that recipe again/Oh no...."

"I may be a dumbass hillbilly," a kid from Arkansas says, "but even I know you don't leave a cake out in the rain. Stupidest thing I ever heard."

"There is no cake," Heinz says. "It is a metaphor." Heinz is a draftee with a college degree. He knows about such things and often shows off his education. (Our drill instructor once said that all college does is make you "more stupider.")

"A what?" asks Arkansas.

"A metaphor," Heinz replies. "A symbol of something else. In this particular instance, the songwriter is referencing a lost love or broken relationship."

"Wait a minute ... wait a minute!" interjects Fulmer, an Okie radio operator. "Does this song have anything to do with pussy?"

Heinz is growing a little exasperated. "Well, maybe ... indirectly. But I wouldn't put it quite that crudely."

"Just as I thought," Fulmer says proudly. "The dude in the song used to get some, but now he's shit out of luck. The cake is a symbol for pussy!" He smiles broadly, pleased with himself, and signals a touchdown.

"What kind of cake is it?" asks Rivera. "Chocolate cake is my favorite. My mom makes the best chocolate cake in the world."

"Come to think of it," another Marine muses, "if I had a choice right now between pussy and cake, I would have to take the cake."

Heinz, his face red as a baboon's ass, looks like he is about to explode. "Guys," he says, as if lecturing a class of first graders. "Guys ... let me explain this one more time. There is *no* cake. There *never* was a cake. For God's sake, forget about the fucking cake...."

The madder he gets, the more we descend into hysterics. My stomach hurts and I can't catch my breath. After a while things settle down. Heinz is the only one not laughing.

"All I know," Rivera says, "is I would sure like to have a piece of chocolate cake right now. Maybe with a little ice cream on it..."

14

GOOD MORNING, VIETNAM!

"I don't want to be the first president to ever lose a war."—Richard M. Nixon

At first light the gun crews on Fire Support Base Alpine are up and beginning another day cleaning cannons, stacking ammo, heating coffee, and listening to the 6:00 a.m. sign-on of Armed Forces Vietnam Radio Network.

"Goooooood Morning, Vietnam! It is time to kick those chickens with some chicken-kickin' music!"

This is always followed by a chorus of good-natured insults by those listening (usually vulgar and explicit sexual suggestions aimed at the announcer), followed by legitimate, heartfelt groans by the black Marines, who genuinely despise country music. Contrary to the movie "Good Morning, Vietnam" with Robin Williams, this morning program is always country music. The sixties rock and roll, which many consider to be the symbol and creative highlight of the decade, comes later in the day.

Days and nights in the FDC bunker run together. Radios squeal static and sometimes the high-pitched voices of forward observers, with small arms fire popping in the background, calling for artillery. The desperate and near-panic voices always put us in high gear in an effort to put rounds downrange as quickly as possible. The words "Marines in trouble," when transmitted to gun crews, never fail to get them scrambling to a rapid and optimal performance level. Once, trying to regain radio contact with one of these frantic voices, there is no answer. The radio operator keeps repeating his call sign, over and over, to no avail. There is nothing but static and silence. The bunker gets deathly quiet as everyone fears the worst. After what seems hours, but is probably only five minutes, the Voice returns.

"Good job," the Voice says (now a couple octaves lower). "Target destroyed. And thank you. *Beaucoup* thanks." In the bunker, the collective sighs of relief are palpable.

One of my jobs is cleaning the Coleman lanterns. I become expert in taking them apart, replacing fuel and nylon mantles, and keeping them burning bright. This is a FNG job, but it's infinitely better than my previous shit-burning duties in the rear. In the bunker I work the maps, calculate ranges, gun angles, and powder charges. There are no days off, no holidays, very little free time. The battery is firing or available to fire twenty-four hours a day. We sleep when we can. The Marines are not as standoffish as they were and I am starting to make friends. I consider myself fortunate. This FDC section does not smoke dope, so neither do I. Although under the circumstances I don't have a lot of moral objections to the practice, I surmise it probably will do little to enhance my potential survival.

Two weeks on Alpine and I get dysentery and shit in my only pair of utility pants. We don't wear underwear ... nobody does. Seeking out the unit's medical Corpsman, he seems to know my problem before I say anything. "Don't tell me," he says. "You have the Screaming Eagle Shits and have shit yourself. Have you been washing your hands?"

I shrug and give him a look of resignation. There is usually no way to wash your hands—or anything else for that matter.

"Well," he continues, "don't worry about it, this happens a lot. Take these pills. You are probably not getting enough sleep. I'll talk to Gunny about giving you some rack time. Take these two Darvons before you lie down. If this doesn't work, look me up."

Back at the bunker, someone hands me a clean pair of jungle pants without saying anything. Apparently Doc had been by with a report. I am starting to *really* like these guys. They seem to look after one another.

One day on the other side of the hill a round explodes in the barrel of one of the howitzers with the 155 battery. Two Marines are killed ... a senseless and terrible waste in a freak accident. Although tragic, they are not from "my" battery. I don't know them and my initial reaction—*At least they were not one of our guys. It could have been worse*—surprises me.

A recon team just west of Alpine is on a night patrol and a Bengal tiger drags a sleeping Marine into the jungle and eats him. (I wonder how the casualty officer explains this to grieving loved ones... "Well, he wasn't actually killed in combat but in a nonhostile event. You see, he was actually killed and eaten by a tiger, but we think it was quick. There are no remains, but we did find some of his personal gear.") Some weeks later another Marine is dragged into a bomb crater by a tiger (maybe the same one, but who knows?), but is saved by his comrades who shoot at the big cat, forcing it to drop the terrified Marine as it slinks quickly back into the jungle.

The all-knowing, all-seeing powers back at headquarters in Quang Tri enlist the aid of a Vietnamese tiger hunter to find and kill the aforementioned animal. Although I don't see him, others say the hunter showed up on the hill via chopper in a white safari suit with a little mutt-looking rat of a dog. The dog is not a tiger killer, or tiger stalker, or tiger hunter. The dog is tiger bait. The hunt is unsuccessful and Great Tiger Hunter catches a chopper back to wherever great tiger hunters live down south.

Later, some grunt on patrol kills a tiger and the carcass is hauled back and strung up at headquarters in Quang Tri. I see pictures and the animal is huge—over four-hundred pounds and nine feet long. Is this the infamous killer tiger? Maybe; maybe not. The officers, cooks and office Marines in the rear take a lot of pictures standing next to the trophy, hung like a sailfish, providing fodder for many exaggerated war stories in letters written home. Nevertheless, no more Marines are attacked and/or consumed.

A month or so later we receive word the battery is moving further north into what some call Injun Country. Closer to the DMZ, more North Vietnamese Army, and a lot more isolated. I get a dark and ominous feeling we are going to assume the same role as the Great Tiger Hunter's little mutt dog.

15

I WILL BE IN
THE AREA ALL DAY

*"I had prayed to God this thing was fiction."—Vanardo Simpson, U.S.
Army Private*

The new fire support base is not anything like I expected, but so
far nothing has been anything like I expected. It is small, and located
on a ridgeline mountaintop with a sheer cliff on the north side. A small
helicopter landing zone is at the highest point and the hill descends
down a hundred yards or so where the six howitzer cannons are positioned. It is called Fire Support Base Neville for reasons I don't know
and never ask. It is destined to be the battery's home for the next few
months.

The rats arrive a couple days after we do. (The North Vietnamese
Army is here already.) Epic battles with the rats begin almost at once.
These are large rats, apparently attracted by the garbage we throw off the
cliff along with our expended brass cannon shells. We club the rats and
stab them and stomp them and mix C-4 plastic explosive with peanut butter in an attempt to poison them, but these rats are aggressive and smart.
If cornered, they will attack. Some Marines claim the rats are trained
agents of the North Vietnamese Army.

One night, wrapped up asleep in a poncho liner, I feel something
warm lying on my chest. It is a curled-up rat, about the size of a half-
grown housecat, and I bounce it off the bunker ceiling. As it scurries out
the door, I unsuccessfully search for something to smash it with, but, like
the NVA, it quickly disappears into the darkness. A couple of Marines are
later bitten by rats and must be sent to the rear for rabies shots. I hear of
one Marine, after we have been here a couple months, who slathers peanut
butter on his toes so a rat can bite him and he can be evacuated. But I

think this probably is just a joke, bantered around by some frustrated artillerymen. At least I hope so.

A new man is transferred to our little Fire Direction Center, but he is not an FNG. Mac, an eighteen-year-old kid from near Chicago, has been with an FO team assigned to the grunts for the last six months. With a mop of curly blonde hair, he looks about fifteen, laughs and smiles a lot, and considers this new assignment a "skate" job. Which, compared to "humping" these jungle mountains with the grunts, I guess it is. We hit it off and team up in a fighting hole down at the perimeter line. We are ordered to report there when the "shit hits the fan."

An understrength company of grunts provides security for the firebase. There are also two mortar crews, a few communication Marines, and our six cannons and crews. Probably a hundred twenty Marines altogether. Maybe less. Although we hold the high ground, it is expected the NVA will eventually mount a ground assault. Already it is probing the lines and our listening posts report movement on a nightly basis. Once, an NVA soldier walks right up to the concertina wire and just stands there. A single enemy mortar round will drop on us at odd times and AK-47 fire erupts at different points up and down the line. Kind of weird ... until you realize it is all with a purpose. The single mortar rounds are fired to determine effective ranges. The other incidents are designed to ferret out our defensive weak spots for the coming assault. It is not a question of if ... only when.

One night there is some small arms fire down on the grunt line. I run down to our assigned hole. A couple minutes later Mac, my new partner, comes tumbling in saying: "Don't bother to come to attention. I will be in the area all day." (This is a standard long-term joke enlisted peons frequently use mocking obnoxious new second lieutenants.) Mac is laughing, seemingly confident and unconcerned. This whole Vietnam experience is a big adventure to him and he is going to have a good time no matter the circumstances. A natural comedian, Mac is his own biggest fan and takes great delight at his jokes. Actually, his jokes are not that funny, but his pleasant and upbeat persona tends to make his laughter contagious. Even the officers grin at his relentless and entertaining bullshit. Mac enlisted just out of high school at seventeen, but the Marines kept him in Okinawa until his eighteenth birthday. The Green Machine does not want any seventeen-year-olds killed in action. It makes for extremely bad press.

"Mac," I say. "Maybe we should put out a couple of claymores [a defensive-type mine that sprays deadly ball bearings that we can detonate from our hole]." To me this is a logical suggestion even though I don't have a whole lot of experience with everyday grunt stuff.

"Hell no!" Mac replies. "The gook bastards sneak up on you in the dark and turn 'em around on you. Then you end up blowing your own shit away and it is *game over.*" He giggles at his own joke. "All we need is frags [grenades]," he continues. "We can chunk frags at 'em and they won't even know exactly where they are coming from. Only fire your rifle if you have to because all the muzzle flash tells 'em is 'Hey, Luke the Gook! We are over here.'" Mac thinks this is funny and laughs again. I guess it *is* kind of funny. Mac's survival skills that he learned so well in the infantry may very well keep us both alive.

As usual, nothing comes of the small arms fire. It is another probe. The NVA, as usual, is in no hurry and is patiently and carefully planning the coming assault. Mac, still chuckling softly to himself, walks with me back to our bunker.

16

A SEXIST PIG

"Freedom is not free, but the U.S. Marine Corps will pay most of your share."—Ned Dolan

Fire Support Base Neville is socked in and has been for almost a month. No supplies, no mail, and all choppers grounded due to the weather. The battery is not firing much because if we can't see anything, nobody else can either. Our radio batteries are quickly losing power and we have used up all the replacements. We are eating some of the more obnoxious C-rations out of necessity. In just a few days, it is determined we will be totally isolated and without any communication at all.

The NVA is becoming more active as the fog and rain allow it to move around unseen and undisturbed. The grunts know this and ask for help in shoring up the perimeter defenses. Three Marines from the FDC, including me, are assigned to stand lines with the grunts. We settle in for the night in a muddy hole near the upper LZ. It is cold, drizzling rain and utterly miserable. We take turns staring into the darkness and fog and imagining NVA rushing us before we even have a chance to respond. In reality, enemy soldiers could walk right up to our hole before we would ever see them.

Through the night one man keeps watch as the other two try to sleep in the bottom of the hole, which is now full of water and mud about three inches deep. There isn't much sleeping and the two men not on watch wrap up with each other in a vain attempt to keep warm. Because the grunts are understandably a little nervous, we don't leave the hole, and piss in empty C-ration cans when the need arises. It is a long night and the worst for me—thus far. Again I am thankful I'm not one of the grunts who must embrace this and similar misery on a daily basis.

Some forty years later, as I listen to the debate about gays in the military

66

and women in combat roles, I often think of this particular night. I would have preferred snuggling up with a young woman Marine in lieu of Thornton, a Georgia boy with halitosis and sour-smelling hair, but I guess you can't have everything. War as a social experiment, I conclude, can become somewhat problematic. Women in foxholes, sometimes for months at a time, with nineteen-year-old horny male Marines? I just do not see how it can work ... most especially in the combat arms units. You may call me a sexist pig if you wish. It is a dumb, unworkable idea, and unfair to all concerned.

A company of grunts carrying fresh radio batteries is dropped about three days out on a rescue resupply mission. The terrain is up and down—difficult on a level just below torture. On the second day, their point man is ambushed and killed and since all the medevac choppers are grounded, they must carry his body the rest of the way. When I hear they are approaching the wire, I walk down to see them. They are exhausted and grim and seem slightly pissed off. Perhaps they think this is our fault somehow. (After all, if we didn't need batteries...) I don't know. None of the grunts is talking. Instinctively, I keep quiet in an effort to show some respect. They are a somber and bedraggled bunch.

Late that afternoon we hear the sounds of a chopper nearby. It is still so foggy the visibility is near zero. One of the newly arrived grunts is "talking in" a medevac chopper to retrieve their dead point man. The pilot, we speculate, must have a "washtub full of balls" because for all practical purposes he is flying totally blind. Someone comments he must be "one of them wild-ass Army warrant officers flying medevac dust-offs." Whoever he is, he hovers just above the cannons at the lower end of the firebase while the grunts lift their fallen brother-in-arms into a Red Cross-marked Huey. The grunts stand quiet in the prop wash. The chopper disappears into the fog, the droning rotors throb and become more and more distant, until finally they fade away.

The next day, or perhaps the day after, the dawn breaks bright blue and crystal clear. No clouds. Not much fog in the surrounding valleys. The resupply helicopters come early, bringing mail, ammo, water and new replacements. And batteries. The choppers continue to come, almost continuously during daylight hours, for the next three days.

17

SHORT-ARM INSPECTION

"The Marines I have seen around the world have the cleanest bodies, the filthiest minds, the highest morale, and the lowest morals of any group of animals I have ever seen. Thank God for the United States Marines Corps!"—Eleanor Roosevelt

Doc, our unit's medical hospital Corpsman, has announced there will be a morning "short-arm inspection" by sections. A short-arm inspection has nothing to do with arms. It is a euphemism for a genital exam to check for lice, crabs, infections and venereal disease. Our FDC section is called as first victims. We assemble in a horizontal line in front of the battery. (It is highly unlikely, I think, anyone will be found with a venereal disease. We have been on a couple of isolated mountaintops for several months.) The officers and staff NCO's do not fall out. Perhaps they have arranged for a private showing at some later time.

"Okay," Doc says, "as I come by, drop your trousers." Nobody wears Skivvies. Like socks, they are uncomfortable, impossible to keep clean, and unobtainable anyway. Doc goes down the line, occasionally lifting things aside with a tongue depressor, looking for ... well, I am not sure exactly. There is a lot of vulgar banter and good-natured insults. The Marines treat this latest indignity as kind of a lark. Most of the comments are directed at Doc.

"Doc," Mac says, "you seem to be enjoying this deal a little too much. I am getting a little nervous." Mac is determined, as usual, to have a good time. Nobody but him could get away with suggesting Doc has homosexual tendencies. Again, Mac's appealing, vibrant and likable personality gives him the leeway to just about say anything. To just about anybody.

"Mac!" Doc replies. "I didn't know you were here. I should have brought some tweezers and a magnifying glass."

Laughter all around. Everyone likes Mac. He laughs more than anybody, as he appreciates a clever and finely tuned retort. Afterwards, Doc gives us a little lecture about keeping our individual bunkers clean of food scraps and garbage. In the war with the rats, Doc explains, "the fucking rats are winning." He says, "I don't want any more of you assholes getting rat bit."

Corpsmen are not Marines, but are part of the Navy. They are attached to Marine units, wear Marine uniforms, and are like paramedics except they can do procedures even paramedics cannot do in civilian life. As one officer put it, "They are long-haired, undisciplined, disrespectful and will run through the flames of hell to help a wounded Marine." Consequently, Marines generally have great fondness for their unit's "Doc." But it comes at a price. No matter the danger or situation, he is honor bound to respond to the words "Corpsman Up!" During the Vietnam War, over 700 U.S. Navy Hospital Corpsmen are killed responding to these very words.

Later, the battery is assigned an additional Corpsman, who is junior to Doc. To keep them straight, the first is henceforth referred to as "Chief Pecker Checker"; the second is stuck with "Assistant Pecker Checker." Both are competent and dedicated and take their new nicknames in stride— not as insults, but as terms of affection. Which is exactly what they are intended to be.

Chief Pecker Checker is a little older than the rest of us and wears wire-rimmed glasses, which make him look like a young country doctor. Usually shirtless, he roams the hill treating everything from cuts to dysentery to NSU. (NSU is nonspecific urethritis akin to the "clap," which is usually caught on trips to Da Nang or other rear areas.) He fusses, cajoles, frets, berates, advises and worries over us like an old mother hen trying to oversee a bunch of wayward and unruly chicks. Everyone likes him, respects him, and his word—at least as far as any medical issues go—is law. He will make a great family doctor in civilian life. I hear that is his ultimate goal after the war.

Around this time I am sent up to the LZ to meet an FNG reporting in one afternoon. New clothes, new boots, and looking well fed, I could have picked him out of any crowd. Remembering my own first days, I try to put him at ease. I wonder if I looked as apprehensive and nervous as he apparently is...

"Welcome to paradise," I say. But as he surveys our somewhat squalid surroundings, he does not seem convinced. "It isn't so bad," I add, "once you get used to it." Helping him with his gear, we start down the hill. Despite myself, I am feeling a little perverse pleasure at his uncomfortableness.

"How long you been here?" he asks, stopping to adjust his pack.

"Five months," I reply.

"You mean you have been *in country* five months?"

"No," I say. "I have been right here for the last five months."

He looks stricken. I regret having felt so smug previously. But he will find his way, just like the rest of us, as he struggles through the first few weeks, makes friends, and becomes part of the unit. Perhaps he will even develop a little pride in being a U.S. Marine in a combat zone. Stranger things have happened.

One afternoon a supply helicopter lowers a cargo net full of ammo and other gear. It also has two insulated thermite containers marked CAUTION: HUMAN BLOOD. Obviously, these are some sort of medical supplies Doc has ordered. We round him up and he seems perplexed. "I didn't order nothing," he says.

On opening the containers we find they are filled with ice cream. Ice cream! A miracle from God, with the help of some sympathetic mess sergeant in the rear. We eat until our bellies are extended and swollen. Many of us are sick for the next day or two. Doc is unhappy but doesn't say anything about our ill-advised and shameless gluttony.

But it was more than worth it. Every ... single ... bite.

18

A MAGIC SHOW

"A casual stroll through the lunatic asylum shows that faith does not prove anything."—Friedrich Nietzsche

"To one who has faith, no explanation is necessary. To one without faith, no explanation is possible."—Thomas Aquinas

A chaplain, along with his enlisted assistant, choppers in one afternoon to LZ Neville and passes the word that services are to be held that afternoon down by the gun pits. Those seeking some spiritual refreshment are encouraged to attend. The assistant, well scrubbed and apparently not having missed too many meals, sets up a makeshift portable altar. Twenty-five or thirty Marines show up, including me.

The chaplain, who seems pleasant enough, gives a short sermon wherein he tries to inject a little humor. The attempt falls flat and he moves on to Holy Communion. A lot of the grunts, mostly Hispanic, line up and kneel to take the sacrament. Right after the short service, the chaplain's assistant packs up the altar and crucifix and they make a hasty retreat. The chaplain is probably a Catholic, but I really don't remember. I do recall a sense of envy for the Hispanic Marines and their apparent simple and unquestioning faith. My own faith, never that strong, has been besieged with doubt and is seriously wavering for several months now.

Back inside our bunker there is an air of vague disappointment. I really don't know what we were expecting. There is probably nothing that the chaplain, who obviously has a difficult job under less-than-favorable circumstances, could say to us to alleviate our unacknowledged and general feeling of angst. But at least, to his credit, he did come out to this miserable place.

"Did you see that chaplain-assistant guy?" Butler asks. "That pogue ass-hole sure has it made. I wonder how a guy could get a skate job like that?"

71

This statement is met immediately by hoots of derision and laughter from the rest of us. Butler is surprised and offended. "What?" he asks. "What is so motherfucking funny?"

"You could never be a chaplain's assistant," someone replies. "You need to get real."

"And why not?" Butler counters. He is genuinely angry at our response.

"Well," another Marine adds, "for one thing, you say the word *motherfucker* way too much. Chaplain's assistants don't talk like that."

"That," says Butler, seething with indignation, "is a motherfucking lie!" We laugh so hard that after a while even Butler joins in.

Botts, a radio operator, interjects that once, back in the "world," he saw Oral Roberts heal a crippled guy. He then proceeds to pantomime the entire sequence of events, playing the part of both the cripple and Oral Roberts. Rolling in on a phantom wheelchair, he looks suspiciously around, tongue poking in cheek, and with a skeptical expression. Oral Roberts lays on a hand (actually Botts' hand on his own forehead) with the command: "Heal! Heal! Stand up and walk!" A natural actor, Botts is convincingly and shakily trying to stand. Wild eyed and teetering, the poor cripple loses his balance, cries "Oh shit," and tumbles unceremoniously to the ground. We laugh like we had good sense and beg him to do it again.

Marines are traditionally known to make the best of bad situations. When bored, we often make our own entertainment whenever possible. A story is going around that we decide to introduce to Mac—the youngest, most naive and innocent of us all. Mac has been away with the grunts for several months and we are confident he is unaware of this particular little practical joke. We begin planning the details before we spring our ambush. A couple nights later during a lull in fire missions in the FDC, the opportunity arises unexpectedly.

Botts, our talented actor, has already been chosen for the lead role. "Did I ever tell you guys," he begins casually, "about that weird-ass whorehouse I went to back on Okinawa?"

Mac perks up immediately, as he has been hardly anywhere and is especially interested in any and all whorehouse tales. The rest of us feign interest in Botts' story.

"Well," he continues, "they had this chimpanzee there and had taught him to shoot pool. He really couldn't play pool, but he could break the balls on the first shot."

"I heard about that place," one of us chimes in as planned. "But I never got a chance to go there." The bait has just been cast. Now it is time to see if Mac will bite.

"Anyway," Botts says, "the girls are all numbered. One to twenty. You pay your money up front and the chimp breaks the balls. If, for example, the number six ball falls in a pocket, you get the girl with the number six. The eleven ball gets you girl eleven. And so on. But the real neat part of the deal is if more than one ball falls. Then you get two girls, maybe even three, for the price of one. A hell of a deal..."

Botts leaves the story there. The rest of us pretend like we are involved in something else. Mac, who has thoroughly bought into the ruse, wants to hear more. A minute or so passes.

"What happens," Mac says, more than just a little interested, "if no balls fall in?"

"Then," Botts says, pausing dramatically, "you have to fuck the monkey."

It takes Mac a few seconds to realize he has been had. He shakes his head as we laugh and then rewards us with what is the biggest and best smile I have ever seen.

19

ANN-MARGRET'S PANTIES

"The most dangerous thing in a combat zone is an officer with a map."—Anonymous

On Christmas Day an Army general choppers in and distributes candy and other little goodies. Apparently he is someone of importance, but I never learn his name. Neither do I care. But I remember thinking there must not be a gook around within fifty miles, otherwise he would never have come. He may have stayed ten minutes; I know it wasn't longer than fifteen. This may be an unfair assessment, but almost never do we see anyone over the rank of captain out where anything is happening. Later this theory is proven wrong on at least one occasion ... but that is another story.

The Marines do not have enough combat billets for all their officers so they are rotated every six months. Six months with a combat unit, then six months in the rear. (There *are* exceptions to this policy.) A combat command is important to an officer's career and it is called "getting your ticket punched." In a grunt or other combat arms unit, the officers come and go. If you are a lowly Marine grunt, however, you spend thirteen months eating out of a can while wet, cold or miserably hot. Sleep, a precious commodity, is limited and comes in uncomfortable, infrequent, brief snatches usually in some nameless shithole hazardous to your health and well-being.

Although I don't remember more than a couple of our artillery officers displaying any outstanding leadership characteristics, neither do I recall any who are totally inept. The battery more or less runs itself as everyone knows his job and does it. The staff NCO's are the frontline supervisors and they make sure things run smoothly. Although it is no doubt a little different in the infantry companies, in our unit officers are more like over-

74

seers on the old plantation. It would be very easy to make further comparisons here about the lower-level enlisted guys in conjunction with the plantation reference, but I will respectfully refrain from doing so...

One day our battery commander, whom we refer to as the Skipper, gives an order that everyone is required to shave on a daily basis. This impresses me as a little ridiculous, because we are filthy and water is in somewhat short supply. I am bitching and moaning about it and the Skipper overhears me.

"Jones," he says, "do you know why you must shave every day?" I am expecting a logical reason that has somehow previously escaped me. "Because," the Skipper continues, "I SAID SO!" (This is the same explanation my mother often gave and is extremely difficult to refute.) The reply I give, with of course a slight variation, is basically the same one I give my mom: "Yes, Sir." This particular issue, I quickly determine, is *not* the beach I wish to die on.

Bob Hope is giving a Christmas show in Da Nang and a drawing is organized to see who gets to go. The officers and staff NCO's do not participate. One enlisted man will be the lucky recipient. It seems that whenever I start developing a case against these authority figures, they do something noble to sabotage my feelings of animosity. Like, on the rare occasions that hot chow is flown in, the lowest ranking man eats first and everyone else follows by rank. The highest ranking officer is the last to eat. I am especially fond of this tradition because as a lowly lance corporal I am usually one of the first in the chow line. In addition, the practice seems to create a little goodwill between the ranks. It is hard to resent an officer or NCO who seems to be providing for your needs before his own.

A rumor begins that at the Bob Hope Christmas Show Ann-Margret (star of stage, screen and the current 1968 sex goddess) prances and dances around the stage in a short skirt sans underwear. Could this possibly be true? A hot topic, we discuss and analyze it from every possible angle. How could a rumor like that get started if there is not some element of truth? Is this just some horny pogue private's wishful fantasy? Is Ann-Margret a pervert and exhibitionist? Is Bob Hope maybe playing "Hide the Salami" with Ann-Margret? And so forth.

"Maybe," says the kid from Arkansas, "the gal just plum forgot to put her drawers on."

This theory is loudly and thoroughly rejected. It is decided that when Sims, our representative at the Da Nang show, returns, we will learn the details of this all-important issue. Discussions of a potential NVA assault, major world events, and R&R have taken a backseat to Ann-Margret's panties ... or lack thereof.

"I was too far back," Sims eventually reports. "So I really couldn't tell." Sensing our disappointment, he continues: "But I talked to a guy stationed there in Da Nang and he had a friend who worked with another guy who said he knew somebody who said he had actually seen a picture. Ann-Margret. Dancing. No underpants."

There it is ... indisputable, photographic proof. We talk about it for weeks.

20

TWO-LEGGED RATS

"First thing I killed was no kind of thing at all. It was an enemy soldier. Which is a lot easier to say than the first thing I ever killed was a man."—Steve Mason

Noises are coming from the trash pit at the bottom of the cliff. Although it is dark, the heavy fog is a more significant problem and popping a flare would be useless. The battery gunnery sergeant arrives and he hears the clanking and rustling among the brass canister shells and garbage.

"Rats," he says after a while. "You guys called me out here for a bunch of rats?"

Gunny is a Korean War veteran and he tends to think we are letting our imaginations run berserk. He is skeptical and unimpressed with mere sounds coming from a trash pit. After Korea, this Vietnam chickenshit experience does not compare with the frozen hell that was his last war.

"I don't know, Gunny," says one of the gun crew. "That is one big-ass rat to be making that much noise."

"Well, okay," Gunny says, exasperated. "If I'm going to get any sleep, maybe we should fire a blooper round down there to shut you guys up." (A blooper gun is an M-79 grenade launcher that fires a 40 millimeter shell that goes "bloop" when shot—hence the name.)

A round is fired into the darkness and fog in the direction of the last noise we heard. There is an explosion and then a high-pitched scream— a sound no rat could ever make. Gunny's eyes get big. *"Damn!"* he says.

"Must be one of them big two-legged rats, Gunny," another one of the gun crew says. Gunny makes no reply. The next morning, the body of an NVA soldier is spotted at the edge of the trash pit. The M-79 round has apparently hit him square in the chest.

A helicopter drops off a new replacement one afternoon. A tall skinny Marine over six feet tall and black as a piece of Kentucky coal, he doesn't walk but kind of floats in a gliding shuffle. Talks in a high-pitched, spooky whisper. His name? Graveyard. I never hear him referred to as anything else but "The Graveyard." "The Graveyard," he will often quote eerily, "don't worry none 'bout dyin', cause the Graveyard is already dead."

I don't know what his job is. I never see him do anything. None of the gun crews want him. Graveyard, a creepy guy, creeps everyone out.

A couple of weeks go by as Graveyard floats, ghostlike, around the hill making spooky-ass comments. The staff NCO's (or somebody) decide to send him back to battalion to work in the mess hall. Much to everyone's relief as the guy is bad for morale with all those "dead and dying" references. We are glad to see him go...

In retrospect, getting sent to the rear was probably his intention all along. Graveyard successfully cons everyone on Fire Support Base Neville. A well played and excellent ruse—unless, of course, Graveyard really *is* already dead.

The South Vietnamese Air Force, flying one of the older helicopters that looks like a big pregnant grasshopper, attempts to land one day on our little landing zone and ends up crashing unceremoniously down by the grunt's perimeter. Nobody is hurt, but the grunts are somewhat perturbed. Actually, they are livid, flat-out pissed. There is some talk about "what these fucking gooks are doing up here anyway." It is South Vietnam's war, but as Americans we have taken ownership of it and resent any interference. Even by the South Vietnamese. As a rule, the grunts have no trust in and little regard for any of the South Vietnamese troops. After all, either from the South or North, "they are all gooks just the same." Weeks drag into months and I find myself developing this same arrogant and illogical attitude. Intellectually I know it is not rational or fair, but on a gut level it is still there.

When I get the chance I hang around the perimeter lines and talk to some of the grunts, more out of curiosity than anything else. Perhaps I am even feeling a little guilty, because compared to them I still have it pretty good. They are standoffish at first, but eventually open up ... a little. (For the most part, they don't associate with, accept or trust anyone but other grunts.) In the daytime they send out a patrol or two, lounge under poncho shelters, play cards, sleep and clean weapons. One story they tell stands out:

"We were on this long hump once. Several weeks. Up and down, raining, so slick and muddy you could hardly walk. Really fucking miserable.

20. Two-Legged Rats

This one kid, after about three days, he starts giving his gear away. C-rations, cigarettes, poncho. Then one day, he just sits down. 'I quit,' he says. Nothing else. 'I quit.' We get ready to move out again and he don't move. Won't even get up. Nobody can get him to move or say anything. Doc checks him out; can't find nothing wrong. The captain comes back from the front of the column, talks to him, even slaps him a couple times and calls him a pussy. That don't work either. We rig up a poncho and start to carry him. No medevac can get in where we are—the weather sucks. Anyway, we carry him about fifteen hundred meters or so, which is hard as hell by the way, and Doc comes back to check on him again. But he is already dead. Dead as hell..."

"What do you think happened?" I ask. "Was he sick?"

"I don't think so," one of the grunts says. "He just gave up ... he just fucking gave up."

On the way back to the FDC bunker a song is playing faintly on someone's battery radio. It is Eric Burton and the Animals: "We gotta get out of this place/If it's the last thing we ever do./We gotta get out of this place/Find a better life for me and you."

21

SMOKING IS HAZARDOUS
TO YOUR HEALTH

"Smoking kills. If you're killed, you have lost a very important part of your life."—Brooke Shields

There are twelve different meals in a case of C-rations. I remember the contents of each and every one of them forty years later. Some meals, like ham and lima beans, are universally despised and are known as "ham and motherfuckers." Other meals, like beans and franks, when mixed with a little tin of cheese are not too disgusting. With few exceptions—such as when in rear areas or the few times "hot chow" is brought out to the firebase—C-rations are all we eat. There are no regular meal times; we eat whenever and wherever we can. Everyone loses weight. Any food care packages from home are routinely shared with fellow Marines. These packages generally don't last a day.

Some meals contain, along with some hard crackers and cheese, a round piece of chocolate wrapped in foil. This particular delicacy is commonly referred to as a "shit disc." Each meal also contains an accessory pack consisting of instant coffee, creamer, sugar, powdered hot chocolate, matches, a small package of toilet paper, two pieces of Chiclet gum, and four cigarettes. Marines who do not smoke sometimes take up the smoking habit out of sheer boredom. Occasionally whole cartons of cigarettes are sent up from the rear to be freely distributed. It seems a little bizarre in retrospect that smoking is not only accepted in Vietnam, but is inadvertently and sometimes even actively encouraged. For some reason, thankfully, I never develop the habit.

In the 1960s the anti-smoking sentiment is just beginning to gain momentum. The surgeon general of the United States requires all packages of cigarettes to display a warning—"Caution: Smoking May Be Hazardous to Your Health." The phrase is a source of great amusement to us Marines. It becomes a long-running joke. Cigarettes may very well be hazardous, but compared to being in Vietnam in 1968 the comparative danger is so far apart to be off the chart and laughable.

So the surgeon general maintains that cigarettes are hazardous to your health. The phrase is excellent fodder for ridicule and sarcasm. Smoking is hazardous? How about incoming mortar rounds? How about snipers? How about man-eating tigers? Some Marines, in the typical gallows' humor of combat troops everywhere, write a new version of the warning on their helmets and flak jackets. "Caution: Vietnam May Be Hazardous to Your Health." Vietnam can not only be hazardous, but the fucking place can also be pretty deadly. And unlike someone who pays the ultimate price after smoking for thirty years, the sometimes fatal consequences of being in Vietnam happen a lot, lot faster.

Pound cake in a can is one of the more popular and palatable C-ration items. Mixed with another can of sliced peaches, it is extremely edible— when compared to just about everything else. Using a small can opener called a P-38 that I carry on a string around my neck, I proceed to expertly open both cans in a matter of seconds. (This learned technique is not that unusual, as after opening several hundred cans even a half-wit gorilla can develop skill and speed.) As I am preparing this cake/fruit concoction one afternoon on FSB Neville, our Gunny interrupts me with some fairly unwelcome news.

"Jones," he deadpans, "I have volunteered you for a water patrol. You are leaving in ten minutes."

I know the weather had us socked in for several weeks, preventing any resupply, but I have never heard of one of these "water patrols." A what? Turns out it is just a patrol to obtain water from a stream near the bottom of the mountain we are occupying as Fire Support Base Neville. Generally we get our water from a tank called a water buffalo which is brought in by chopper. The buffalo's belly has been bone dry now for several days. One more thing the choppers are not able to deliver is something far worse than dying from thirst. We've had no mail for almost a month now.

Water patrol sounds dangerous to me. We know the entire area is infested with gooks trying their best to kill us and vice-versa. "I am not a grunt," I tell Gunny, "so I don't do patrols. Plus, I don't ever remember volunteering. Besides, this whole deal sounds like it may be hazardous to my health..."

Gunny ignores me as by this time I have already established myself as an outspoken but somewhat likeable smart-ass. Even as I am saying this, I know I am wasting my breath. No one takes my protestations seriously. Not even me. I know I will have to go.

"The grunts will be going with you to help provide security," Gunny replies, failing to acknowledge a single word I just said. "You don't have to do anything but help carry the water back up. Now get your gear together."

Ten minutes later, with around fifteen other Marines, including five grunts, we head down a steep, slick mountain trail with empty five-gallon water cans en route to a stream several hundred meters below. It is tough going, even though the water cans are empty. It gets worse.

A photographer comes along with us. I don't know if he is a Marine combat photographer or from one of the major news agencies, but he is treated somewhat shabbily by everyone. I am not sure why, exactly, other than we have the feeling he is there by choice, in contrast to the rest of us. Apparently he actually did "volunteer" to go with us. Idiot. What a fool. I have the impression he is hoping something combat related will happen so he can get some good "action type" photos. I pray he will be hugely disappointed. If we are fast and quiet enough, we can get in and out and the NVA will be totally unaware of our presence. No one talks to him and he stays off by himself like some kind of untouchable pariah as we fill the cans in the stream. I note that the little twerp is not even carrying a weapon. I guess if we are ambushed he will depend on the rest of us to save his picture-taking ass.

Going back up the mountain, now with full five-gallon cans, is difficult and exhausting. Carrying the awkward military containers, I never realized that just five gallons of water can be so heavy. Several Marines slip, fall and slide precariously back down the steep trail before being stopped by other members of the group. For the first time in my Vietnam tour I am envious of the five grunts who accompany us on this so-called patrol. They are not required to carry any of the rock-heavy, muscle-numbing water cans.

It takes us all afternoon to get back up to the firebase. As we finally straggle clumsily through the wire, the squalid sand-bagged bunkers and two barrels of smoldering, nose-burning shit at the firebase resemble and smell a lot like an exotic Shangri-La. The place has never looked better.

It sure is nice to be home.

CHIEF

On mail call days
the photographs I share
of new cars and picnics,
smiling blue-eyed people
eating wedding cake
are always returned
without comment.
Chief never gets any mail.
Never.
He eats sliced peaches,
C-ration apricots and pears,
while I sort stacks of perfumed letters.
"Got any pineapple bits?"
He knows the answer.
I always steal
more from supply
than I can eat.

22

BOB'S WIFE

"I get mail; therefore I am."—Scott Adams

The red nylon bags full of mail and packages sustain us and prevent what would otherwise be an inevitable descent into some of our darker and more unpleasant mental places. Mail from home keeps us sane and hopeful, and is often able to right a listing and sinking psychological ship. The mere sight of a Marine running off the back of a chopper with one of those red bags full of mail is uplifting—the ultimate morale booster. Occasionally a few weeks will go by with no mail, but generally the Marines attempt to get our mail to us as quickly as possible. Sometimes the weather, but more oftentimes the war, interferes with timely mail delivery. But under the circumstances, I always felt those in authority generally do the best they can.

My mother writes two or three times a week and sends a package at least every month, sometimes more. Sardines in mustard sauce, Kool-Aid, Vienna sausages, cans of spaghetti, smoked oysters, and the like. Any cookies or other homemade baked items arrive as crumbs, which we distribute and eat anyway. A couple of girls from high school write to me a time or two, but then fall by the wayside. Out of sight … etc. I am gone for much too long. Two years is an eternity for an eighteen-year-old girl. My seven-year-old sister writes and even sometimes sends pictures she has drawn and/or colored. ("Dear Bill, I was in the Christmas play at church. I was an angel. But my wings got crooked.") Sometimes, when mail is delayed, I will get a big stack of letters all at once. I habitually arrange them in dated order and just read one or two a day.

During my time in Vietnam, Mom relates that my dad drives from his job in town to the family farm during his lunch break to check for mail. Every day! He's looking for a letter from me. The longer between letters, the more they both worry. Once, around my birthday, I get a letter from Dad. I recognize his careful and neat block-lettered handwriting on the envelope immediately. It is the only letter he ever writes to me. I can't remember much about the contents. Now I wish I had saved it.

Once, towards the end of my tour, the mail is delayed for three weeks. One day up on the DMZ, I am suddenly overwhelmed with a surreal feeling that something has happened to my dad. Actually, it is a lot more than just a "feeling." Something has happened—of this I am quite sure. I do not think he has died, but I instinctively know something significant and not necessarily good is taking place. A week or so later a letter from Mom explains that on the very day I had this rather unusual premonition, Dad had some major emergency surgery. ESP? Coincidence? Bullshit? All I know is that it happened.

In thinking about Dad I remember as a kid how women act around him, especially when Mom is not around. To a young boy the women all seem to act a little nonplused and slightly "goofy" in his presence. There's a lot of smiling, giggling, blushing and exaggerated head tilting. I am not able to understand it fully till after I hit puberty, after which the explanation becomes quite clear. Up into his forties, Dad is over six feet, has a head of wavy jet-black hair, and piercing blue eyes. Great physical shape. Movie-star good looks similar to the actor Tyrone Power. Once I see a young woman look at him, gasp, and scream in delight. These reactions seem to amuse him. To my knowledge, he never did figure it out. Or if he did, he never responded to any of it.

Bob, a Marine radio operator from Ohio, spends a lot of time with us maintaining the communications in the FDC bunker. Like my dad, he is a good-looking, square-jawed athlete type who could easily be a male fashion model. Perhaps only two things could hinder a possible successful career in the fashion industry. On one forearm Bob has a large tattoo of the Marine's symbolic trademark—the eagle, globe and anchor. (Bob refers to it as the buzzard, ball and chain.) On the other forearm he has a big yellow tattoo of the cartoon character Tweetie Bird, with the inscription "I Tought I Taw a Putty Tat" underneath it. To Bob this little witticism is the apex of cleverness, although I will grudgingly admit I never saw another tattoo quite like it. Before or since.

Bob is a good radio operator and has an upbeat and extremely pleasant personality. Kind of like the personality you would expect anyone with a Tweetie Bird tattoo to have. There is one flaw, however, in Bob's otherwise exceptional performance of his radioman duties. Sometimes one of the enemy, a North Vietnamese Army soldier, will somehow acquire one of our radios and attempt to talk to us. The standard procedure is to ignore the transmission so the enemy soldier would think he is not being received and eventually abandon the effort. The Vietnamese-flavored accent always gives them away. For example, our call sign at one time is something like "Grasshopper Two/Four." Generally, an Oriental person cannot say Grasshopper Two/Four with an American accent. It comes out as "Grass-a-hop-pah Tu Fo." Bob always loses it at this point and initiates a long profanity-filled harangue at the offending enemy soldier. Which, of course, just makes things worse. We always end up having to change the radio frequencies.

One evening Bob shows up at our little bunker with a borrowed battery recorder and a cassette tape from his wife. "You guys shut the fuck up," he says, "and let's listen to this." The young woman's soft, pleasant voice soon fills the bunker, talking of mundane things—a missed anniversary, a phone call from his parents, a shopping trip to a nearby town. She then talks of her longing and loneliness, and the monologue begins to have some slight sexual overtones. Nothing graphic, just some one-sided "pillow talk" between a husband and wife. The rest of the Marines are quiet, maybe a little uncomfortable with eavesdropping on a private and intimate, perhaps even slightly sacred, conversation. In the half-light I think I see Bob's eyes glistening. If Bob feels any embarrassment, he does not show it. I suppose he feels that if we share everything else we can share this too. But, none too soon, the tape comes to an end and nobody knows what to say. Almost anything would be inappropriate. Bob breaks the silence after a couple of awkward minutes. "Well," he says, upbeat as ever. "How about that shit!"

That night I wrap up in a poncho line and unsuccessfully try to sleep. Usually sleep is not a problem, but tonight I toss and turn with a vague uneasiness. An unsettling emotion with a tinge of homesickness permeates my efforts. It takes a while before I realize the source of my unexplained insomnia.

I am missing Bob's wife.

23

MORE LIKE
AN EARTHWORM

"Only imbeciles and fools fight fair, and won't do so for long."—Marine saying

Every night the battery fires what is called "harassing and interdiction" rounds at predetermined areas in the surrounding jungle. These are speculative targets, usually picked by an officer, where the NVA is thought to congregate. That is ... maybe congregate; or maybe not. Thousands and thousands of high-explosive artillery shells are expended trying to wild-ass guess where the NVA might be. It is akin to picking the winning number in the lottery, but with far less chance of coming even remotely close. After several months I begin to think perhaps all our efforts in Vietnam, however good intentioned, are essentially and simply a fool's errand. To my knowledge, for example, our unit never does kill any NVA with this expensive and foolhardy game of chance.

Why, I wonder, do we not attempt to confront and engage the NVA where we know for certain it is? Laos, Cambodia, North Vietnam. But the answer further supports my darker suspicions. The NVA can cross any border at will; we are not permitted to do so. There are other restrictive and foolish rules of engagement as well, although we are the only side required, or even attempting, to follow them.

The NVA travels as light infantry and chooses when and where it is to its advantage to attack and ambush us. Its troops know the jungle well (it is, after all, their home) and they can retreat when necessary to predetermined safe havens. They can move fast with stealth, cunning and expertise and are in this thing for the long haul. In contrast, we Americans want a quick victory so we can pack up and go home. NVA troops know all our positions. We generally have no idea where they are. They slip

88

silently through the jungle like wisps of fog, patiently waiting for the most opportune times to engage us. In contrast, an American infantry company moving noisily through the jungle is like the Ringling Brothers Barnum and Bailey Circus come to town.

Mac, my partner and friend, is a little upset. He is scheduled to go on R&R in a month or so and everyone has been ordered to get a haircut. The Skipper obtains some primitive-looking manual hand clippers from somewhere and passes the word. (In the Skipper's defense, I suppose we all are looking a little shabby.) Mac has curly blonde hair and speculates a shorn head will inhibit his ability to get laid on his upcoming trip to an Oriental nookie factory.

"I guess," Mac says sadly, stirring a C-ration can of beans and franks, "I will have to go on R&R looking like a bald dickhead. Just my luck. I might as well stay here with you assholes. I got about the same chance of getting laid right here." Mac is acting like a kid who has just been told Santa Clause has been killed in a tragic sleigh accident and Christmas has been postponed—indefinitely.

"Mac," says Arkansas, who has recently returned from Bangkok. "Mac, you are worrying about the wrong thing. Just make sure you take enough money for a week or so. These girls ain't concerned with anything but what you have in your wallet. Don't sweat it. *Beaucoup boom-boom.* You will be just fine ... as long as you have a little money. Forget about your hair, for God's sake. Your hair ain't got nothing to do with it. Hair or no hair, when you get back from R&R you will be completely *fuck foundered.*"

The explanation seems to give Mac some hope. As a result of this little pep talk, his ever-present smile starts to return.

"But, come to think of it," Arkansas adds, "before you leave you might want to borrow Doc's tweezers and magnifying glass." (Mac is still being teased about his encounter with Chief Pecker Checker.) Mac, a kid who is impossible to insult, doubles up in a little fit of laughter, along with the rest of us.

We have previously interrogated Arkansas about every facet of his whoring and debauchery in Bangkok and he is happy to oblige in providing lurid details. He, a country farm boy, describes Bangkok as a state fair, "except they have girls!" At least some of the stories, exotic and borderline pornographic fantasies, are probably true. At least we all hope they are.

The topic quickly shifts to sex and a couple of the stories sound suspiciously similar to accounts I have read in letters to *Penthouse* magazine. They usually go something like this, with only slight variations: "I was home alone one Saturday afternoon and a big bus stalls in front of my house. It just so happens it's a women's Swedish Bikini Swim Team and it will be several hours before a rescue bus arrives. Well, my air conditioner is on the fritz, but I invite them into the house to wait for the new bus. These are tall blond beautiful girls with hard swimmer's bodies. Hot as it is, they start shedding their clothes..."

When you don't have any sexual history, or at best a limited and pathetic one, it behooves you to try to make something up. Especially when in the company of lonely nineteen-year-old Marines a long, long way from home.

Most of the Marines, including me, do not have a lot of stories about sexual escapades. We are all too young to have experienced much of anything. As Michael Herr, author of the book "Dispatches" writes: "Vietnam is what we had in place of happy childhoods." To those of us who survive, the war will remain the most memorable and significant event of our lives.

Mac is telling a story about his high school girlfriend. Too young and inexperienced to even fabricate a realistic story, he relates the nearest thing he can think of that might qualify as a sexual event. "I never could get her to do anything," he complains about the young girl who no doubt is the first and only girlfriend he ever had. "She regarded my wiener as some sort of poisonous snake."

"More like an earthworm," someone interjects. "And a little one at that."

"Well," Mac continues, ignoring the barb. "I finally came up with a plan. If I could just get her to realize it wouldn't bite, maybe we could start from there. At the movies I got a big box of popcorn that we shared. She keeps reaching in to get a handful. When she wasn't looking, I slip the ol' wiener up through the bottom of the box." By this time Mac, as usual, is laughing so hard at his own story that he can no longer continue. Although we suspect the story is probably unadulterated bullshit, we all laugh along with him just as much.

The next day Gunny tells us the latest scoop from battalion headquarters. Half the battery—which consists of three cannons and their crews, three Marines from the FDC, two officers, and Assistant Pecker Checker—are moving to a hill just south of the old Khe Sanh Combat Base. I am on the list to move. Mac is staying.

23. More Like an Earthworm

In effect, we will be dividing our forces in exactly half. I seem to recall something like this happened once previously in our country's history. Something about an epic and extremely lopsided battle that occurs near the Little Big Horn.

24

FRIENDLY FIRE

"Life is full of misery, loneliness and suffering—and it's over much too soon."—Woody Allen

The battery is assigned temporarily to Vandegrift Combat Base (VCB) prior to being assigned to another firebase. It is a hub of activity with units coming and going from various operations all across Vietnam's I Corps. It is 1969 and the war, despite what General Westmoreland says, does not seem to be going well. The NVA, at least in the northern part of South Vietnam, seems to operate freely and can more or less go anywhere it so desires. The Tet Offensive, along with the Khe Sanh debacle, has somewhat soured the American people and the voices of opposition on America's home front are growing louder ... and stronger.

The battle for the old imperial city of Hue (pronounced "Way") in February 1968 is especially shocking to American sensibilities. A turning point, some will later say. In this, the first television war, Americans trying to eat their meatloaf and mashed potatoes are bombarded nightly with images of chaos, napalm, and dead and dying U.S. Marines and Vietnamese civilians. Actual street fighting—urban combat—filmed by some very brave camera crews, bears little resemblance to movies and television shows. I was never in Hue, but knew several Marines who were there prior to the savage battle that lasts twenty-six days. Every Marine I talk to says it was a beautiful and ancient city. "Was" is the operant word here. "Rubble" would be the most descriptive adjective used after the battle. Although the Americans prevail, Tet is the beginning of the end to America's adventure, or perhaps, misadventure, in Vietnam.

Initially the Marines mount an unsuccessful attack on Hue with two understrength infantry companies, facing approximately ten thousand entrenched North Vietnamese Army regulars and Popular Liberation

24. Friendly Fire

Forces. At first our general officers, miles away and in the luxury and comfort of the rear, simply do not believe the enemy can possibly field that many troops to defend the city. Marines are the best infantry in the world, but not against these type odds. The Marines, unprepared and ill trained for house-to-house combat, are making it up as they go along. During the early days of the battle the rules of engagement prohibit the use of artillery and airstrikes. Without reinforcements and a change in tactics or altering the absurd rules of engagement, no doubt we would still be there in a stalemate with a determined North Vietnamese Army. Afterwards, thousands of Hue residents are discovered rotting in mass graves. All have been executed by communist forces as "collaborators" with the United States and Vietnamese governments. The local populace refuses to help the invading communist forces. Mistakenly, the well-trained and fiercely dedicated invaders anticipate that the people of Hue will happily join them in a revolutionary uprising. But the population does not help the Marines either. Like most of the Vietnamese people, more than anything they just want to be left alone.

The estimate of enemy forces killed is somewhere over eight thousand. During the battle about three thousand Vietnamese locals are also killed by the communists. Total civilian casualties are estimated as at least ten thousand. Many are killed by our forces due to several hundreds of artillery and airstrikes, as these are the days before "smart bombs." The South Vietnamese Army (ARVN) is also a participant, but casualty figures for it are somewhat elusive. It is almost as if the South Vietnamese Army is so unimportant nobody thinks to write down its combat losses. (I am sure there probably are some elite and aggressive ARVN soldiers, but I never see any.) American losses? Two hundred fifty-two killed in action and over fifteen hundred wounded—in less than a month. Primarily Marines and Corpsmen, plus more than a few U.S. Army guys. I don't really know what the U.S. Army is doing there. Advisors to the ARVN, perhaps, or part of the hastily sent reinforcement troops. Maybe a blocking force. Whatever the reason, I am sure the Marines are glad to see them. In the end the city of Hue is virtually destroyed.

We win the battle, but lose the war.

The Skipper gets drunk one night and wanders around the gun emplacements encouraging his Marines to fire into the darkness. Nobody pays any attention to him. On a previous occasion on LZ Neville, he also gets hammered and enters into a brawl with the X.O. (executive officer) and one of the staff NCO's. Neither incident elevates my confidence in his competence or my respect for him as our superior officer. But his six-month combat tour will be up soon and he will rotate back to the rear. Another officer will arrive to take his place and to get his career ticket punched.

The battery is kind of "standing down" and the VCB area is reasonably secure—if there is, in fact, such a condition that exists in Vietnam. One evening, two black Marines from one of the guns are singing and their rich, full baritone voices float across the valley. It is a melancholy tune with lyrics that resonate with loss and hope and loneliness. The song is "Daddy's Home" and I remember the words almost fifty years later:

"You're my love, you're my angel
You're the girl of my dreams
I'd like to thank you for waiting patiently
Daddy's home.... Your daddy's home to stay."

The command element of the battery, along with the FDC, is headquartered in a tent. As the song continues, a couple of my Marines (who I know are married and have kids) clear their throats and walk outside to hide their misty-eyed emotions. Music, I quickly conclude, does indeed soothe the savage beast.

On radio watch one night an artillery round screams over the top of the tent and explodes behind us, setting off an inferno of stored fuel drums. Mortars are bad enough but these big arty rounds are far more destructive and scare the hell out of everybody. In what can be described as a moment of wild and sheer panic, we run from the tent for a nearby trench and pile on top of one another. After a few minutes it seems there are no more rounds on the way and nobody is hurt, so we amble back to the tent.

"Who has radio watch?" the Skipper asks. (He is the first one in the trench.)

"I do, Sir," I answer. I am wondering where this is going.

"Well," the Skipper says, "you left your post. You should never leave your post."

I don't answer or even attempt to defend myself. Perhaps I should have said I was following my commanding officer's lead, but there is no way I would have stayed exposed in the tent, alone, while everyone else bolted and sought cover. It is not mentioned again.

The single artillery round, we find out later, has been fired from a U.S. Army battery some miles away. "Friendly fire," it is determined, although once again it does not seem all that friendly to me. (They need to come up with a more appropriate name for these catastrophic errors.) We curse the Army as incompetent "dogfaces," but our battery is guilty of the same offense some months before—only with far more tragic results. A short round, fired in error by one of our guns, kills several Marines. The baby-faced gun crew chief responsible, a young kid who didn't want the job in the first place, is so utterly destroyed by the incident that he is sent to the rear. I don't know what happened to him or if he faced any charges as a result of this sad affair, because we never see him again. Completely devastated, the kid is obviously grief stricken and will carry his mistake with him to his grave. An accurate figure of Americans killed by these so-called friendly fire incidents in this strange and confusing war with no front lines will probably never be known.

A USO show is held several days later on an improvised stage. Two- to three-hundred Marines, mostly grunts, assemble on a hillside that serves as an amphitheater. The band is from Australia and when three round-eyed, short-skirted women appear, there is a thunderous roar of approval and genuine surprise. Round-eyed women! Scantily clad beauties! Here? In this shithole in the middle of nowhere? This is unquestionably some kind of miracle.

The band leads off with a song popular at the time: Archie Bell and the Drells with "Tighten Up." Many of the black Marines, some of whom no doubt have not heard any music at all for months, simply cannot contain their joy. They stand up and begin dancing with unbridled enthusiasm. Halfway through the song a 122 millimeter rocket hisses in and explodes a couple hundred yards away. Even from a distance, I can tell the dancing girls are shaking with fright. They are hustled toward a waiting helicopter. This is not something they signed up for...

The Marines clap and cheer and encourage the USO troop to take the stage again. Reluctant and trembling, they return and attempt to start over. The next rocket lands right behind the stage. They run to the waiting chopper this time and are all too soon just a memory—although an extremely short and very pleasant one.

Two black Marines, who have tripped up running for cover, are rolling on the ground laughing at this latest turn of events. As I pass I hear one of them say: "Sheeet, ain't this some bullshit. Least little sign of trouble and the bitches *sky* out."

25

REGRETS

"It was never easy to guess the ages for Marines at Khe Sanh since nothing like youth lasted in their faces for very long."—Michel Herr, "Dispatches"

"When you are at the Khe Sanh Combat Base," a Marine general comments, "you're really not anywhere. You could lose it and you really haven't lost a damn thing." Isolated and vulnerable, the base is difficult to resupply, and living conditions are deplorable. Nevertheless, General Westmoreland, commander of U.S. forces in Vietnam, considers Khe Sanh to be "of vital strategic importance." President Lyndon Johnson says the base should be held "at all costs."

The six thousand Marines at Khe Sanh, a corrugated airstrip surrounded by bunkers and trenches, pay a heavy price for this policy. In a single day during the Siege of Khe Sanh, over a thousand rounds of enemy heavy artillery pound the base. It is reported that over two hundred Marines lose their lives. But some military historians dispute this figure. Counting the Marines killed in plane crashes and defending the base on surrounding hills just before, during and after the infamous siege, they estimate that well over a thousand Marines are killed in action.

Khe Sanh Combat Base is abandoned less than a year later, no longer considered to be of any strategic significance—if, in fact, it ever was. The NVA decides it wants no part of it either and also retreats. All that remains is the steel matting of the runway stretching along the red clay valley floor. Along with a company of grunts, our three howitzers are now positioned on a hill overlooking the metal airstrip. Khe Sanh Combat Base is destined to become hallowed ground ... another legend in Marine Corps history and lore. Since we are on an artillery fire support base that has been recently abandoned, the bunkers are thankfully already in place. So are the rats.

25. Regrets

Hutch, the forward observer fighting his own private war, shows up unexpectedly here on what was formerly called FSB Cates. It is still a great mystery, to me and most everyone else, how it appears he comes and goes more or less as he pleases. There is a rumor that on a previous combat operation, Hutch climbs a tree in order to better adjust artillery on the enemy. Over six hundred NVA are allegedly killed as a result of his actions. I have no idea if this is true, but nobody questions it and nobody asks him about it.

"My business is killing," Hutch says with his characteristic toothy grin. "And business is good!"

There is another story, somewhat more credible, about Hutch in a bunker with sleeping Marines. Upset with the rats scurrying around in the darkness, he begins blasting away at them with his pistol. Nobody is hurt and the story simply adds to his growing reputation. "Hutch," the Marines say admirably, "is one crazy fucker." In war, insanity and bravery are often indistinguishable from one another. In the upside down world of combat, strange and eccentric behavior is sometimes overlooked. Oftentimes it is the fearless actions of the crazy ones that will keep you alive.

Late one night in a musty bunker Marines are talking about regrets. There are the usual stories of failed and broken relationships, missed opportunities, poor choices, and other events common to most young American males. But surprisingly no one voices any regrets about being in the Marine Corps. Despite our present circumstances, the Marines have given us a sense of purpose and belonging and pride which many have never felt before. It has nothing to do with the legitimacy of a dubious and mismanaged war in Southeast Asia. It is the sense of camaraderie that is seductive, intoxicating and memorable. And although we do not realize it at the time, it is something we will never experience again...

At age twenty, my personal regrets are minor and virtually insignificant. Like Frank Sinatra, I have a few, "but then again too few to mention." The big ones are to come later. One regret I had at the time was my unwillingness to help a friend being physically abused during infantry training by an NCO called a "troop handler." These are not drill instructors, but Vietnam infantry veterans who vary in temperament from dedicated to indifferent to sadistic. Although no doubt I would have paid a price, I should have intervened, despite any potential personal consequences. There is an element of cowardice here that plays havoc with my self-concept. Intimidated and frightened, I did absolutely nothing. Nobody else in the company did anything either, but that does not alleviate a nagging sense of personal shame.

Hutch sits quietly listening to our adolescent ramblings without comment. Someone asks if he has any regrets. "Only one," he says. He then proceeds with the following story:

"We were on this company size Op and already got into the shit a couple of times. A lot of gooks we walked into that we didn't know were even there. One guy in the company was a real shitbird. I caught him asleep on watch a couple of times. Everybody is tired but he thinks he can put everybody's ass on the line. I told him if I caught him asleep once more he was going to pay a price he really didn't want to pay. Sure enough, that night I was checking lines and found him asleep in his hole. I went a little crazy. Pulled him out and started beating him and could not stop. He cried and begged and sobbed like a whiney little bitch. I finally got so tired I couldn't hit him anymore..." Hutch gets quiet for a couple minutes.

"I guess that is my biggest regret. I know now I should have killed the bastard."

26

Bad News

"Hell is empty and all the devils are here."—William Shakespeare

Less than a month after the battery is split in two the long-awaited ground assault comes to LZ Neville. Nobody is surprised. The news comes in bits and pieces as we listen to garbled and somewhat confusing transmissions on the radio's battalion frequency. It doesn't sound good. We huddle silently in a bunker several miles away and anxiously await information. Another firebase, LZ Russell, located just east of Neville, is manned by another of our battalion's artillery batteries and is attacked at the same time. This adds to the chaos amid the frantic voices we hear from both places on the radio.

Over two hundred North Vietnamese Army regulars from its 246th Regiment storm Neville's understrength position on this February night. Preceded by a devastating mortar attack, the Marines retreat to the safety of their bunkers. Other NVA troops known as "sappers" have breached the perimeter wire and are crisscrossing the hill, throwing chicom grenades and satchel charges into bunkers and gun pits. For all practical purposes, the firebase has been lost, but a couple of staff NCO's rally the remaining Marines for a counterattack and by the next morning the position is more or less secured. "They threw their best at us," one Marine says later. "But we still came out on top in the end."

There follows numerous stories of heroics and sacrifice. Several NVA soldiers, wounded but still alive, are hung up in the concertina wire surrounding the hill. The situation is still unstable and a gunnery sergeant, citing the need to conserve ammo, makes his rounds with a K-bar knife and methodically slits their throats. The grunt company commander (so I am told) finds an NVA wounded officer and shoots him between the eyes with his pistol. The first and only rule of close combat, I am to discover, is ... well, there are no rules. It is open season, no bag limit, with suffering and death the byproduct and end result. It is difficult to describe the rage, grief and sense of helplessness in these situations. Add a little bitterness and the toxic combination is "life changing." The attack that night on LZ Neville certainly changed mine. And I wasn't even there.

The next day we find out the full impact of the previous night's events. Fire Support Base Russell has reported twenty-nine Marines KIA (killed in action). It's a stunning revelation, as it is doubtful there are more than one hundred Marines there all total. One of the Marines there I know from artillery school—a big, friendly kid from somewhere in North Dakota, and I remember hoping he survived. Later I learn he did not.

The casualty figures from LZ Neville are not quite so shocking number-wise, but they are nevertheless just as catastrophic to us. The figure is fourteen Marines dead and no count on the wounded. We get a list of the KIA names via radio. Most of them are grunts, killed in their fighting holes during the attack, and although I know many by sight, I don't recognize their names. Then some all-too-familiar names are read at the end of the list:

Barret, a corporal and gun crew chief whom I had a little minor dispute with as an FNG. Entirely my fault, I was getting in the way around his gun and he rather impolitely and rudely corrected my "unwelcome" presence. On the back of his flak jacket he had written "When I Kill All I Feel Is Recoil." As this was his second tour, I remember thinking he should have never come back. Don't guess he is feeling anything now. Later, I hear the poor guy does not die a quick or painless death.

Doc, our Chief Pecker Checker. Everybody loved Doc. A gentle and caring guy, he did his best to take care of us. He is killed looking out for his Marines. Somehow, I know he would not have wanted to go out any other way. Our remaining Corpsman, his good friend Assistant Pecker Checker, is especially devastated by the news. As are we all.

Mac. This name is followed by a rush of anguish, grief and suffocating sadness. Not Mac. Anybody but Mac. The youngest and best of us, he is our precocious little brother looking forward to R&R. Mac is much too innocent and good-hearted and this simply cannot be true. But of course it is.

There are no tears, at least no visible ones. We are numb with anger and shock and grief. The tears will come later. Sometimes, even almost fifty years later, they still do.

27

IN COUNTRY R&R

"I am a member of the Vietnam generation. I did not serve."—Al Franken

In the dream I am on an inflatable air mattress being swept out to the South China Sea, out of the war and into a dimly lit and uncertain future. Suddenly awake, I realize it is not a dream after all. I *am* on a rubber air mattress floating in the South China Sea, but fortunately only a hundred yards or so from shore. How did I get here? Where is my rifle? Where are my Marines?

The reality comes to me in pieces, rising slowly from a mental mist, but still a little unfocused. The day before, my artillery battery boards a Navy landing craft on the Cua Viet River en route to a three-day "in-country" rest and recreation facility. The beach, designated for this purpose, is on the coast of South Vietnam near the mouth of the river. I recall that the boat ride is a pleasant and relaxing experience. The countryside is beautiful, despite all our constant and relentless compulsion to blow up the fucking place. The whole experience seems surreal. Jungle firebase one day; cavorting on the beach the next. Despite my best efforts, I simply cannot remember exactly when, in relationship to my year's tour, this happened. Neither can I remember where we came from or where we went after the beer fest and swim party. There is plenty of cold beer, steaks, and a cheesy USO show by a Korean band replete with a bevy of short-skirted dancers. The event is probably after the battery rejoined, as I recall some Marines from the tragedy at LZ Neville were there. Others, obviously including Mac, the Chief Pecker Checker, Barret and several wounded, were not. But I could be wrong. After fifty years, I suppose it really does not make any difference.

There are no women sunning themselves on the expansive white sand beach. The Marines all wear G.I.-issue boxer underwear in lieu of swim trunks. There are some Vietnamese women hanging outside the concertina wire surrounding the camp. Peasant women in black pajamas, all their teeth are stained black from chewing betel nut—a Vietnamese habit of the poorer classes. Their personal hygiene, I would guess, is about what you would expect from people in a Third World country with no plumbing. Nonetheless, the rumor spreads that several Marines were caught having sex with them through the wire. I have no idea if this is true, but it occurs to me that this level of desperate depravity is something I want to avoid. But who knows? Too long here and everyone changes, not necessarily for the better. Already through this war I have discovered things about myself I would be better off not knowing...

One night, I remember, I was assigned perimeter guard duty with two other Marines from a different unit. They had some dope, most likely bought from the concertina women, and invite me to join them in getting stoned. Does everyone in this miserable country smoke marijuana? I decline and stay up most of the night. Although this R&R spot seems reasonably safe, I am beginning to think there is not really any safe area in this entire country. I imagine those black-toothed concertina women slinking through the wire with satchel charges.

I get an e-mail some forty-five years after returning home: "Is this Bill Jones, former Marine from Golf Battery?" Well, yes. (Who could this be? A reporter investigating reports of a North Vietnamese scalp? A relative of some killed-in-action fellow Marine?)

It turns out to be from Wayne Hicks, an old friend from my unit who found me on social media. On LZ Neville we share a two-man bunker down by the perimeter wire. Wayne is a draftee and artist with a wife and a baby on the way back in Minnesota. In what little free time we have he continually draws in a sketchbook that he carries around. I am extremely pleased to learn he has had a successful art career and a family after the war. A talented and super nice guy, he has no business in Vietnam. But, then again, neither do the rest of us.

Wayne sends me pictures of our time in the Cua Viet R&R camp. Four of us from the FDC are on the beach next to a pyramid of empty beer cans. Our smiles look a little forced. Were we ever that young? And were we ever that thin? One photo is of a young skinny kid with glasses staring somberly into the South China Sea. It takes a few seconds before I realize it is me.

Wayne was with the half battery that was overrun on LZ Neville during the time we lost our friends. In all our correspondence, he never mentions it.

And I never ask him anything about it.

28

LZ SITTING DUCK

*"If during a firefight you see two colonels conferring, you likely have
fallen back a little too far."—Unknown Marine grunt*

March 1969. Operation Purple Martin. Who thinks up these names?
It sounds like a bird-watching excursion. We should have known something was up. Back at battalion headquarters there are clean clothes, showers, beer and steak at the mess hall. The scuttlebutt is we are going to a
place called LZ Argonne, just east of the border with Laos and a little
south of the DMZ. Some Marines, in the fashion of our typical gallows
humor, have renamed it "LZ Sitting Duck."

The NCO's make sure we have plenty of personal ammo. This is a bit
unusual and we suspect they know something the rest of us don't. I put
together fourteen loaded magazines and stuff a bandolier with seven frag-
mentation grenades. We are encouraged to take as much as we think we
can carry. This latest move seems curiously different, for reasons difficult
to pinpoint. An air of foreboding surrounds the men of the battery, akin
perhaps to someone facing major surgery. There is a sense of dread cou-
pled with stoic resolve. The men are unusually quiet as we board several
twin-rotor choppers and head west to the Laotian border.

We begin our descent onto a smoke-filled hill and the two machine
gunners begin firing in long bursts from each side of the helicopter. (I am
thinking that coming into an LZ is a strange place for them to be test firing
their weapons. The capacity of a human being at self-deception, I later
conclude, is limitless.) Out of a side window I note that one helicopter has
already landed at the top of the hill, but the rotors are not turning. Strange,
I think, for it to just sit there exposed...

We land at the bottom of the hill and run off the back ramp. Along
with my FDC buddy Riles, we are carrying a wooden ammo box full of

View from "grave" fighting hole at LZ Argonne, March 1969.

charts, maps and other gear. Our assignment is to establish a Fire Direction Center at the top of the hill. A mortar round lands a few feet behind the chopper, which is already lifting off. Riles looks okay and I surprisingly don't see any blood coming from me. The round is close and at least one of us should have been hit. A grunt at the edge of the little LZ is firing furiously into the nearby jungle. I don't see anything, but then again you almost never do. Grunts spend a great deal of their time firing at trees in the jungle. And these particular trees are shooting back.

We start up the hill and more mortars fall, but not nearly as close as that first one. In addition, supersonic bumblebees are whizzing around amidst this unbelievable noisy and confused chaos. Somebody in those trees, I think somewhat incredulously, is shooting at me and Riles. Riles apparently reaches that same conclusion at the same time and we collapse in a hole a few feet away. The hole is already occupied by a young redheaded grunt. By his clothes and new boots he is obviously an FNG and could not possibly have been in country more than a couple of weeks. He is also newly dead, having caught a round directly between his eyes, most probably one intended for us...

"Don't look at him," Riles says. "Don't look at him and don't think about it. We need to get going." Riles is a lot braver than me. I would have been content to spend the rest of the war in the relative safety of that hole. Soon we are at the top of the hill next to the disabled Huey full of holes and blood that we saw on the way in. The dead and wounded Marines have already been removed. The two machine guns on either side are also missing. Someone says the NVA waited for the chopper to land and then raked it with automatic weapons fire. A discarded, shattered and gore-filled flight helmet indicates that at least one of the pilots was killed. I don't know who got the machine guns, but hope it is not the gooks.

Most people live out their lives, in the words of the poet, in "quiet desperation," without really being afraid. Not just anxious, nervous, concerned, upset or a little worried, but flat-out convinced your life is about to be over ... soon. A fear that is palpable, consuming, debilitating, drying your mouth, constricting your throat, and immobilizing your limbs. Thanks to Riles, the fear does not overwhelm and leave me frozen to the extent that I cannot function. But there is definitely some beginning frostbite and it is spreading rapidly. The fear does not win ... this time. But it comes close. Real close. Entirely too close.

We make it to the top of the hill and begin organizing our maps and charts in an abandoned bunker. From the time we leave the hole with the dead grunt till we reach the crest of the hill is a total blank slate. I have no memory of how we got there. None.

29

PLAYBOY FOLDOUT

"The rank stench of those bodies haunts me still
And I remember things I'd best forget."
—Siegfried Sassoon, World War I poet

The grunt battalion commander on LZ Argonne, a lieutenant colonel, along with one of his staff NCO's, is killed on the first day. Or maybe it is the second day. Nevertheless, he doesn't last long, which is the very reason we seldom if ever see any higher ranking officers in positions of great danger. But at least this particular officer is down among his troops and not flying safely overhead barking orders at semi-panicked lieutenants and captains. Although he is killed about forty yards from me, I do not see it happen or even hear about it till later. Such is the pervasive element of confusion and lack of information in combat environments. Apparently an old-style World War II–type gung-ho Marine officer, his death causes me to reconsider my cynical attitude toward those Marines in high-ranking leadership positions. This officer has balls and is with *his* Marines. As he should be. Unfortunately, he is the exception, rather than the rule.

A couple of NVA soldiers are dead in a hole next to the downed chopper and a few feet from the bunker Riles and I have just occupied. One of them has a foldout picture from a *Playboy* magazine in his pocket—no doubt some jerk-off material—and the discovery infuriates me. This close to Laos and the DMZ, there is no way he could have obtained that picture except by going through the gear and/or pockets of a dead Marine. There are also a couple of letters, in Vietnamese, which I take and keep for several years. At the time, the grim irony of this situation escapes me...

Doc, who is now "Chief Pecker Checker" since the death of our other Doc and friend, pulls the bodies (now beginning to stink) down the hill a little ways and sets them on fire. Their fighting hole, about the size of a six-foot-long grave, I quickly claim as my new home. It's a little messy, but one can't be too choosy. Inside I find a couple of NVA-issued freeze-dried rations that look to be just as good as anything the Marines have, but I throw them away because they are "gook food." The two bodies, along with some others, burn and smolder until the day we finally leave ... almost two weeks later.

Our dead and wounded are having a difficult time being evacuated because the choppers are taking too much fire coming into the landing zone at the bottom of the hill. For our dead this obviously does not matter, but the poncho-wrapped bodies lined up at the bottom of the hill are somewhat of a troubling morale issue. At least for me. I try not to look down there. Our three cannons are in position now and we begin to initiate fire missions. Soon we are nearly out of ammo. And water. The resupply choppers have stopped coming ... the LZ is much too "hot."

To solve the ammo problem, large pallets of 105 howitzer shells and mortar rounds are parachuted onto the hill. This does not go well. The chutes miss the hill and drift leisurely off into the jungle. The NVA's mortars are 82 millimeter in size, whereas our mortars are 81 millimeters. The gooks can use our ammo in their mortar tubes, but their rounds will not fit in ours. For the next several days, we are mortared with what is most probably our own ammunition—which we conveniently supply. Air strikes are called in to try to blow up the ammo pallets before the gooks get them, but this is only partially successful. Sending out patrols to retrieve the ammo is simply out of the question; there are too many NVA out there in all directions. They surround us.

We can hear when the gooks drop a mortar round in their tubes. It makes a distinctive sound that sends everyone scrambling frantically for cover. Since this is a previously abandoned firebase, they don't have to fire any "adjustment" rounds. The first round is always on target and they are more than a little proficient. A good mortar crew (and admittedly these NVA crews are extremely good) can get a number of rounds in the air before the first one ever hits. I resolve that at my first opportunity I am going to make my new home mortar proof. Under these circumstances, the former gook hole is starting to resemble a grave a little too much for my liking.

After a couple of days it suddenly occurs to me that unless things start to change pretty quickly, we may not make it off this godforsaken hill. Later, I think it somewhat curious that this thought contains the pronoun "we," not "I."

30

A GOOK KILLING MACHINE

"Generally speaking, the way of the warrior is resolute acceptance of death."—Miyamoto Musashi

LZ Argonne had been occupied some months before, so there is still junk around that will be beneficial in fortifying my new residence. I find a piece of steel airplane matting and drag it over to the top of my hole/grave and place a couple layers of sandbags over the metal sheet for good measure. A couple of sniper rounds buzz nearby, but not that close. I surmise that as long as I keep moving, the chances of being hit are fairly minimal. It is the mortars that are the biggest, most lethal danger and the source of my gut-wrenching fear. Unless a lucky mortar round happens to fall in my two-foot hole entrance, I will be reasonably safe. That is, if not caught out in the open like the hapless grunt commander.

The Skipper is in the FDC bunker a few feet away. He eyes my new fortification. "Nice hole you got there, Jones," he says in a friendly manner. "Real nice."

"Thank you, Sir," I reply. "I have been working pretty hard on it." I do not volunteer that the reason for my ball-busting industry is that I am scared shitless. These gook mortars, I think, are eventually going to kill us all.

"You know," the Skipper continues, "that hole, being close to the FDC and all, would make a nice home base for your battery commander."

So, I think, there is a reason for this little social chitchat. I should have known. "Well, Sir," I counter, "this is my hole. I guess you will have to find your own."

The Skipper then laughs like the whole conversation is a joke, but we both know it is not a joke. And I quickly resolve that I will not give up the

109

hole without doing ... something. What, I don't know. But apparently the Skipper has second thoughts about confiscating my fortified grave and drops the issue.

Later I think about how intimidated I was not that long ago when I watched a troop handler sergeant beat a friend with a tree limb in infantry school. Now I more or less told a captain (respectfully) to go fuck himself. Amazing what a few months in Vietnam can do, especially when survival becomes part of the equation. I often wonder what I would have done if the Skipper had in fact ordered me out of my little fortress. In reality, probably nothing.

The mortars are falling again, kawumping outside our flimsy bunker as we take cover inside. Trying to make myself as small as possible inside my flak jacket and helmet, I look across at the Marine squatting across from me. He has a leather shoulder holster with a .45 caliber pistol. The holster is unusual—I have never seen one up to now. When I look at his face I realize it is the supply sergeant from back at battalion. This explains the holster. The supply guys get all the good stuff before anyone else.

"Sarge," I say between explosions, "what are you doing here?"

"Well, I heard you guys were in the shit. So I hitched a ride with a medevac and came on up."

Wow! Apparently, he does this on his own. It is not something I would have done. I mentally forgive him for scarfing the holster—even if he is in a rear area. The dude is very brave or else a damn fool. (The distinction is often impossible to determine.) Anyway, my estimation of the guy immediately spikes hundreds of points. This Marine Corps mentality is hard to explain ... Semper Fi.

That afternoon some NVA troops are spotted running around on the hill a few hundred yards west of us just inside the border with Laos. The FDC Gunny, my immediate supervisor who seldom if ever leaves the safety of the bunker, happens to be outside and quickly takes charge of a gun crew. Ordering the crew to swing the cannon around and lower the tube for direct fire, he shouts encouragement, makes elevation adjustments, and pours high-explosive rounds into the gook position. "Willie Peter!" he yells. "Burn them!" Willie Peter is the term for white phosphorous shells that are banned to use in this fashion by the Geneva Convention. Gunny apparently has not heard of this rule, or if he did he does not care. Neither do I, nor any of the rest of us fighting for our lives on this isolated, very small hill. Watching Gunny take command and work his expertise, I swell with a somewhat surprising sense of pride. This is *my* Gunny. And he is a gook killing machine.

Hutch comes walking up from the other side of the hill. We are surprised to see him; he didn't come with us. Apparently he hitched a ride with one of the first arriving grunt platoons. Smiling broadly, he is in great spirits despite the obvious and dire predicament we now find ourselves in. He's a man in his element, confident and self-assured. And still crazy.

"We killed some gooks on the other side of the hill," Hutch relates excitedly to me. "Do you want to go see them?" I shake my head no. I have already seen enough dead gooks.

"One of them," he continues, "is a woman. A gook nurse or something. Maybe," he adds with a knowing wink, "she is still warm."

Hutch laughs at his little joke and seems slightly amused at my reaction. Up to this point I considered myself to be kind of shock proof. But a woman? We are killing women now? This is not something I had even imagined up until today, as this far north all we ever encounter is North Vietnamese Army regulars. Unlike the Marines fighting down south, there are no kids, no old men, no women. Until now.

Hutch, I conclude, has been here too long. The war has damaged him—possibly beyond any hope of redemption. I feel a little sorry for him. How, if in fact he does survive, can he ever go home and live in the suburbs, work a regular job, go shopping at the mall with his wife, take his kids to Little League practice? The war has robbed him of any decency, humanity or compassion. And perhaps even his very soul.

Later, actually many years later, I realize that war damages everyone in one way or another. Even the ones who do not go...

The extent of the damage is simply a matter of degrees.

31

GRAND THEFT AUTO

"When soldiers have been baptized in the fire of a battlefield, they have all one rank in my eyes."—Napoleon Bonaparte

As far as officers go, Lt. Kegel is not too bad. Actually, he is more than a little decent. I wish more of our officers were like him. A stout little fireplug of a man from Pennsylvania, he comes to us from a tour with the grunts. Why he is assigned to us and not in the rear I don't know, but he is reasonable, competent and laughs a lot. A letter home to my folks says my lieutenant is "okay," and he "doesn't think he is Jesus Christ." We all like him. I don't think he and the Skipper get along, but they keep any disagreements they may have private. Officers stick together, even if they hate one another.

"Kegel," the lieutenant explains, "is the same name given to a gynecologic exercise doctors have women do to tighten up their snatches. I am proud and honored to have the same name as this important and truly wonderful medical technique." This warped sense of humor may have something to do with Lt. Kegel's popularity with his Marines. Also, from what we hear on the lance corporal grapevine, our lieutenant also has a pair of brass balls. For action while previously serving with a grunt unit, we hear he is up for a Silver Star. One long night, bored and hunkering in a bunker, I ask him about it.

"Well," he says reluctantly, "it was kind of an accident. We are assaulting this hill and I have a grenade in each hand. I have already pulled the pins and threw them away. Anyway, once we got to the top nothing is going on and I have these two frags with no pins ... a fine mess I have got myself into. So I throw them in what I think is an empty bunker where they explode. But guess what? There happens to be some gooks in there!" No doubt this is bullshit and does not remotely resemble the truth. Even

112

if he is an officer, he doesn't take himself too seriously and is an extremely likable guy...

For the first few days on LZ Argonne the airstrikes are continuous during daylight hours. The fighter jets, in radio parlance called "fast movers," put on quite an impressive show all around our position. Roaring in from different directions, they skillfully drop high explosives and silver tumbling canisters of fiery orange napalm. I am especially fond of the napalm because being overrun in a ground attack is a real possibility and the more NVA who are fried (converted involuntarily to "crispy critters"), the more it increases our odds for survival and significantly lowers the enemy's chances ... a lot. Thank God for Dow Chemical.

One day an F-4 "Phantom" fighter drops all his ordinance in several passes and comes screaming low level over the top of our hill in a final run. He is doing at least four hundred knots or more before he climbs almost straight up, doing a "victory" role before returning to his base. Apparently he knows we have our collective asses in a sling and this last gesture is a tribute of sorts. I like to think this is probably a Marine fighter pilot, but don't really know. I don't suppose it matters. Nevertheless, it is a goose-bump producing, inspiring and unforgettable moment.

After about three days the airstrikes have suppressed incoming mortar fire enough to allow the resupply choppers to bring ammo, water and supplies, and to evacuate the dead and wounded. The water situation is approaching the critical stage and many of us suffer from dehydration. The water arrives none too soon. Lt. Kegel asks (i.e., *orders*) Clapton and me to stack some newly arrived wooden crates of 105 millimeter ammo in a nearby big trench. Clapton is a communication guy but his real love involves, as he says, "blowing shit up." On his own, he has hung around and helped the combat engineers enough that he knows more about explosives than they do. Whenever the battery needs something blown to smithereens, Clapton is our man.

As we work, Clapton regales me with stories of his previous life in Houston, Texas, as a professional car thief. According to him, he stole hundreds of cars and never came close to being caught.

"What about the cops?" I ask. "You never worried about the police?"

Clapton replies with a snorting, derisive laugh. The question amuses him. "The cops only catch you if you're stupid," he explains. "You can't go joyriding around in a car you just ripped off. The key is you got to unload it quick." He then gives me a tutorial about the little tricks and intricacies of grand theft auto. Experience is the best teacher and obviously Clapton has had a lot of firsthand experience.

"I don't know," I say. "It seems pretty dangerous to me."

Clapton looks around and spreads out his arms. Here we are in a hole stacking up high explosives waiting for the next round of gook mortars. *Dangerous?* We both realize the ridiculousness of our situation and laugh simultaneously.

"Anyway," Clapton continues, "this shit sandwich we are in now has made me think a lot. When I get back, my life is going to change ... big time." (I am thinking that perhaps he is going to begin a life of service to others, or perhaps he has had a spiritual epiphany and may even consider entering the ministry. After all, war changes people.)

"From now on," Clapton explains, "all I steal is high-end vehicles—Corvettes, Jaguars, Mercedes. Fuck them Fifty-nine Plymouths."

The mortars begin falling a few moments later. Clapton doesn't like our proximity to the ammo and runs to find a safer hole. These gook mortar men are good, too good, and most probably are targeting this stack of artillery shells. At first I elect to take my chances in the trench, but on an unexplainable impulse decide to follow Clapton. A few moments later a mortar round hits exactly where we both were standing. It misses us by less than thirty seconds.

There is some sort of frenzied commotion a few yards away near the FDC bunker. From the sound and tone of voices, I know something tragic has happened.

Something really bad.

32

FIX BAYONETS

"Life, to be sure,
Is nothing much to lose,
But young men think it is,
And we were young."
—A. E. Houseman

After the mortars stop falling I hear someone yelling. The voice sounds like Hutch. Running back to the FDC bunker, I see Hutch, distraught and weeping, running around in a little circle. "The Big O is dead!" he is saying, over and over. "The Big O is dead!" A Marine is prone at his feet, not moving, with a hole in the back of his flak jacket the size of a dinner plate. A mortar round has fallen directly into his foxhole, a few feet from mine, killing him instantly. There is nothing anyone can do.

I do not know the dead Marine, a radio operator with the nickname "the Big O" who is just getting back for a second tour. Hutch and this unfortunate dead guy apparently have a history. (This is another Marine, I think, who should never have come back. You can only dodge the bullet so many times.) Hutch quickly composes himself and calls for a poncho to carry his dead friend down to the LZ. There are no ponchos—we have already used them all on the dead and wounded. Hutch's voice becomes cold, menacing and clear. "I want a poncho," he says evenly, "and I want one *now!*"

Ponchos start appearing from all directions. The Skipper comes running up with a poncho in an outstretched hand saying, "Here, Hutch, take my poncho."

I grab one corner of the poncho and we start carrying the Marine down to where his body can be evacuated. It is uneven ground with a heavy, shifting load. One Marine, an FNG, drops his corner and so we pick up and start again. A few more steps and the FNG, who no doubt is having a difficult time with this grim scenario, drops his end again. Hutch looks at him steadily and says, "You drop him one more time and I will kill you." I believe him. Apparently so does the FNG, because we stumble shakily down the hill without any further incidents.

LZ Neville and LZ Russell are both overrun some three weeks prior to our arrival at Argonne. We anticipate quite logically that the NVA will attempt the same tactic here. In my one-man hole, I fashion a little dirt shelf near the entrance and stack some frag grenades with the pins straightened for easy pulling. Mac, my young fighting-hole partner on Neville, has taught me well. I wish he was here with me. Tragically, he apparently fails to follow his own advice and leaves our perimeter hole on Neville during the ground assault to go to the aid of a wounded comrade. I learn that Mac is killed by an enemy Chicom grenade. The grenade explodes next to a barrel of aircraft fuel and he is incinerated beyond recognition. In fact, during the confusing aftermath of the assault, it takes a couple days to determine that it is indeed Mac.

God, I miss that kid. I miss his upbeat sense of humor and his laugh and his willingness to help out anyone without hesitation. Which, ironically, is exactly the attribute that gets him killed. But more than anything I miss his youthful attitude and unshakable conviction that somehow, even in the midst of seemingly impossible circumstances, everything is going to turn out just fine.

At dusk, standing in the entrance of my hole, an incoming 122 millimeter rocket hisses a few feet overhead and slams into the bottom of the hill where the dead NVA soldiers are burning. It is a huge explosion, and it is close. There is no way any of our bunkers, including my steel-roofed tomb, can take a direct hit from one of these.

"If the gooks start dropping in the heavy shit," Lt. Kegel says with his characteristic grin, "we are all fucked." That night, expecting a major ground assault, the word is passed to "fix bayonets." Fix bayonets? I can hardly believe my own ears. It is a phrase I have only heard once before, in a movie. But thankfully there is no ground attack, that night or any other night, probably because we leave before the NVA can organize one. And although we still get the mortars (thanks to us, the gooks still have plenty of mortar ammunition), there are no more of the big asshole-puckering rockets.

There *is* a dead, putrid smell in my hole. Lighting a match, I find a piece of scalp, still with a shock of black hair, embedded in the dirt wall.

32. Fix Bayonets

It is from one of the NVA soldiers we set on fire. (I hope it is the one who had the *Playboy* foldout in his pocket.) In a flash of creative genius—or, on reflection, perhaps depravity—I dry it out the next day in the sun, attach a string to it, and proudly display my "scalp." This is met with great amusement by my fellow Marines, who regard it as the ultimate souvenir and/or good luck charm. No one gives the slightest indication that this is not civilized or acceptable behavior. It is simply a minor diversion. As I write this now in the comfort of an air-conditioned office, this morbid little incident seems unbelievable to me—almost like it happened to someone else, someone from the past I don't really know and don't even like very much. But then again I suppose denial, as is often said, is not just a river in Egypt. There is simply no rational excuse for barbarism—for me or anyone else. Even while wading waist deep in the middle of a brutal and foolish barbaric war.

Hutch is wandering around the hill with binoculars looking for artillery target opportunities and nearby gooks to blow up. It is his calling, his reason for being, his purpose for living. He seems to have recovered quickly from the death of the Big O. Or at least I think so, until he puts a pair of lace bikini panties sent to him in the mail by his girlfriend over his head and starts walking casually around with them as he looks through their leg holes. No one, not even the officers, say a word to him.

I think he may be losing his mind.

Near Laos

Just outside the wire
a recon patrol walks
almost jauntily
into an L-shaped ambush.
Automatic weapons pop
and in between staccato bursts
high-pitched voices scream for salvation.
"Come on," Hutch says.
"We got to help them."

33

SHOW HIM THE SCALP

"There is no rectitude whatsoever. There is no virtue. As a first rule of thumb, therefore, you can tell a true war story by its absolute and uncompromising allegiance to obscenity and evil."—Tim O'Brien

It is the third day on LZ Argonne and still no water resupply. I am assigned to guard our remaining half-full five-gallon can at the entrance of our FDC bunker. In the middle of the night, with everyone else sleeping and me on radio watch, a Marine crawls up to the entrance. A grunt, he has no weapon, flak jacket, or helmet. There is an unmistakable look of desperation, fear and something else on his face I can't quite describe.

"You got water?" he croaks. The guy is so thirsty he can hardly talk.

"I got a little," I say. "But I am not allowed to give any out." He looks at me without changing expression. I think the conversation is over, but he apparently does not. The stare down continues.

"Okay," I say, "one cup, but don't tell anyone." He nods and drinks a canteen cup in two gulps before slithering off into the darkness. I hope he doesn't spread the word to his grunt friends, as I know if they show up I will give water to them all. And face any consequences in the morning.

If he had only argued a little, it would have been easy to turn him down. Something about his "look" got me. No doubt the guy has been through a shit storm the last few days, along with his fellow grunt brothers. How could you refuse anyone, especially these exhausted and hollow-eyed infantrymen, a cup of water?

The next day Hutch, using a field radio (called a Prick-25), is casually adjusting artillery on a gook position located on a nearby hill. Leaning against his pack, he might as well be ordering a pizza. Calling for some delayed fuses, the impacting rounds penetrate deep in the earth before exploding. There are several secondary explosions—an indication it is a direct hit on a gook ammo supply. "Good job," Hutch tells the distant bat-

The Body Burning Detail

Left to right: L/Cpl. Jones, Lt. Kegel, L/Cpl. Thacker, L/Cpl. Risk. No one smiling on return from Operation Purple Martin.

tery. "You guys were right on it." It is uncanny how Hutch can ferret out these gooks and their hiding places. Just another day at the office.

Watching Hutch, I am suddenly overwhelmed by a strange sense of peace and well-being. It is somewhat of a spiritual experience, a transcendental moment, a surrender of will and the ever-present instinct of self-preservation. Whatever happens is going to happen. There is nothing I can do about any of it. Life is a dream; we are foolish to think we have control. For a twenty-year-old, I think I have had a pretty good run, more than Mac, and I am grateful and content. It is an unexpectedly unique, fleeting, but very real and powerful emotion. It passes all too soon...

Two Marines on one of our cannons are wounded one afternoon and are brought down into the FDC bunker to wait for a medevac chopper. It is surprising that more of the gun crews are not hit, as they are out in the open, completely exposed when returning fire, humping ammo, and working fire missions. In the FDC bunker, we are safe as in our mothers' arms— relatively speaking. I would not want to trade places with these cannon cockers, or anyone else stuck on this meat grinder of a hill.

One of the Marines is hit in the hand and he is rocking back and forth. Obviously it is extremely painful and he curses anyone of Oriental heritage loudly and continuously until someone finally tells him to give it a rest. The other Marine, Rivera, has a head wound and he stares off quietly into space. I ask him how he is doing. He looks curiously at me like he has never seen me before in his life. No answer. Several months later I will meet him under entirely different and somewhat odd circumstances.

33. *Show Him the Scalp*

There is a considerable amount of small arms fire erupting just down the hill. A grunt patrol has been ambushed just outside the wire and is calling for help. Why they ever went out in the first place is beyond me—everyone knows the gooks have us surrounded. But the grunts, as is their nature, go out looking for trouble. They find it soon enough.

"Come on," Hutch says to me, "we got to go help."

Selfishly I think, they got themselves into this fix and they need to get themselves out. The self-preservation instinct has once again unashamedly surfaced more powerful than ever. Nevertheless, I follow Hutch.

Someone yells "gas!" This is my chance to weasel out. The automatic weapons fire is popping louder and more intensely than ever. I don't have a gas mask. Lost it months ago. I never heard of the gooks using tear gas previously.

"Hutch!" I shout, stopping on our descent down the hill. "I can't go ... no mask." A panicked Marine is running by us, gas mask in hand. Hutch snatches it from him and tosses it to me. No excuses now. Fear has blossomed from a small flame to a roaring, almost uncontrollable fire. The fear is winning and rapidly consuming me. I stop again.

"I can't go, Hutch. I just can't go."

Hutch looks at me briefly, more with a look of surprise than anything else. He doesn't say anything, but continues on his own toward the crescendo of gunfire. In a brief moment I decide to follow. No matter what happens, there is no way I want to live with Hutch's haunting look of surprise.

There is no tear gas. We help drag a dying black Marine, gut shot and moaning piteously, back up the hill to safety. (Years later I read that one of these Marines is awarded the Medal of Honor. His picture looks like this same kid, but I cannot be sure.) Hutch never mentions my cowardly reluctance to assist those hapless Marines in trouble. To me or to anyone else.

After ten days Fire Support Base Argonne is abandoned for the second time in less than a year. An article later in the *Stars and Stripes* newspaper says the operation is a huge success, with light casualties. It fails to distinguish which side, us or the gooks, is the successful participant.

We board big Chinook Army helicopters for the ride to join the other half of our battery on a firebase further south. We are unshaven, stinking, filthy and almost giddy with relief—glad to be alive. I am sitting next to one of the Army crew's machine gunners. One of the FDC Marines elbows me. "Show him your scalp!" he yells over the aircraft noise. (Word of the scalp has made me somewhat of a morbid minor celebrity.) I hold up the scalp by the string and the gunner smiles and gives me a thumbs-up. Suddenly a revelation washes over me like warm water.

I am turning into Hutch.

34

CHIEF

"Take me to the brig. I want to see the 'real Marines.'"—Lewis "Chesty" Puller, Marine General

Chief, a member of the Hopi tribe from Arizona, has been in the Marine Corps for over five years but is still a private. Although he has been promoted numerous times, a running battle with alcohol has consistently sabotaged his hope of keeping any stripes. Chief doesn't care about stripes or the increased responsibility the stripes represent. A likeable and competent Marine, his fellow cannoneers tease him about "hogging all the fucking rank."

On LZ Neville one of my duties is sometimes distributing the mail. Chief never gets any mail. *Never.* I wonder about his background and attempt to engage him in conversation by showing him photographs of birthday parties and weddings sent to me from my family. Smiling middle-class white people having a good time. A strange and different world. Examining the snapshots carefully and with genuine interest, he hands them back. "Wow," he says. Nothing more. Just "Wow."

In the days before the term "Native Americans" became politically correct, all American Indians in the Marines were nicknamed "Chief." The naive rationalization, I suppose, is that all American Indians aspire to someday be chief. Illogical and a little silly, perhaps, but there is no derogatory connotation intended or implied. Although from a different culture, the "warrior" ethos inherent in their histories is somewhat consistent with that of the Marines. It is a good and natural fit.

Coming from the South, I know little about tribal differences. When I first meet Chief, I innocently ask him if he is an Apache. It is the only tribe name I can remember.

"Apache?" he replies, his smiling moon face instantly collapsing into

125

a frown. "I am not Apache. Apaches are renegades and thieves. I am Hopi." The response is similar to what I envision would occur if I had called one of my black Marine friends a "nigger." I make a mental note to not bring it up again.

One night on LZ Neville, Chief gets rip-roaring drunk on some smuggled whiskey and decides he has had about enough of this Vietnam bullshit. "Fuck this place," he says while putting on his pack and gathering his gear. "I'm going back to the reservation."

A powerful and barrel-chested man, the fight is on. Eventually members of his gun crew subdue him and prevent what no doubt would be his tragic and certain demise if he had ventured beyond the firebase perimeter. To my knowledge, the officers and staff NCO's never learn of this incident. Even if they do, there is a good possibility nothing would be done. What could they do? Chief is already just a private. And he is otherwise an outstanding Marine and valuable member of a gun crew.

Between operations we are back at Quang Tri headquarters and Chief is very drunk ... again. Passed out and sprawled across a large spare truck tire, he has on a pair of headphones listening to his favorite song, "Ina-Gadda-Da-Vida." The pounding drum solo, of which he is especially fond, is turned up so loud that even we can hear it. The next morning a hung-over Chief grins sheepishly. "Last night," he explains, "the Iron Butterfly kicked my ass."

When LZ Neville is overrun and Barret is wounded and dying in a gun pit, Chief volunteers to go get him. The gooks use Barret as bait and shower grenades on anyone attempting to render aid. Chief takes a piece of tarp, crawls out, and drags Barret back. On the way he picks up a couple of enemy Chicom grenades and throws them before they explode. Barret dies the next morning as the incoming medevac chopper thumps toward the beleaguered firebase in the fog.

Chief is awarded the Silver Star for his actions. If he had been an officer rather than a slick-sleeved private with a colorful service record of nonjudicial punishments and demotions, his heroics would probably be Medal of Honor material. But Chief has no interest in stripes or medals or any of the trappings of this "stupid-ass white-man's war." Sent to Hong Kong on R&R, he gets drunk and goes AWOL. After a little time in the brig, he is back with us—still a private.

Chief likes C-ration pineapple bits and I try to save some for him every chance I get. He looks me up when he gets back from his little R&R

adventure. "You got some piney bits?" he asks. I have several cans and he beams in gratitude. It occurs to me suddenly that the blood of those ancient Arizona warriors still courses through his veins.

"You know, Chief," I say, "that was a brave thing you did with Barret."

"What," he asks, somewhat perplexed. "You know he died?"

"I know. But that is still a really brave thing you did."

"Well, I didn't know he was going to die. Maybe if I knew that, I wouldn't do it."

35

REMF's

"If the rear echelon troops are really happy, the frontline troops probably do not have what they need."—Anonymous

Singapore. It is the only R&R space available but it does not matter because I would have gone anywhere. A chopper brings me back to the battalion headquarters and from there I catch a little "flying boxcar" C-123 to Da Nang for a commercial flight on to Singapore. It seems strange to be back in what could be called semi-civilization. The next few days are destined to be even stranger.

One little incident has remained with me for over forty years. Waiting for the flight from Quang Tri to Da Nang, a sergeant is writing our names down on a clipboard for the flight manifest. If the plane fails to reach Da Nang, authorities will at least know who is/was aboard. It's logical enough, but especially important in a war zone.

A grunt, apparently just in from the "bush," walks up to the makeshift counter where the sergeant is writing. The grunt, a big black guy in full battle rattle, is next in line. How, you may ask, do I know he is a grunt? That's a good question. I really don't know other than he has that "grunt" look. The next thing that happens, however, confirms my earlier suspicions.

I am reclining on some boxes watching sidelong this little one-act play. The sergeant glances up at the grunt and says gruffly, "Take off that bandolier of frags. You can't take those on the aircraft." The grunt—who has been through who knows what, but no doubt nothing remotely pleasant—stares menacingly at the sergeant and doesn't move. The homicidal look he gives the clipboard-wielding sergeant scares me a little, and I am just a spectator. Looking up from the clipboard, the sergeant is obviously taken aback. "Please?" he adds, in a much softer tone. "If you don't mind."

A full ten or fifteen seconds later, much to everyone's collective relief, he hands over the frags.

The base at Da Nang is a small city with almost all of a small city's amenities. Beautiful Vietnamese women, many of them half–French as a result of France's ill-fated previous experience in Indochina, stroll leisurely around, sometimes in the company of Americans. These French/Vietnamese young women are drop-dead gorgeous. Many people are in civilian clothes and some of the Vietnamese women are wearing the pretty, traditional pastel silk outfits that look something like sophisticated pantsuits. Marines diddy-bop around unarmed. They act like they are on vacation at a beach resort. In fact, there is a beach—China Beach, not very far away—that caters to primarily pogues and officers. There are a lot of air-conditioned buildings, ice cream stands, a bowling alley, and the large Post Exchange is well stocked with anything you could possibly want, like stereos, cameras, and jewelry. You can even buy a new automobile there and have it waiting for you on your state-side return. As the saying goes: "War is good for business—invest your son." Since the Vietnam War, we have evolved as a society. Now, because women are a significant and important part of America's military, I suppose we must add "or your daughter" to this phrase.

The rear, full of REMF's (rear echelon mother fuckers), is light-years away from anything I have seen before. There are two distinct wars being fought; the combat arms troops are in one war and everybody else is in the other one. There are nine support troops for every Marine assigned to one of the combat units. At Da Nang, many of the black Marines are infatuated with the "Black Power" movement prevalent in the late 1960s. They walk around like wolves in packs of three or four and when meeting other African American Marines engage in a ritual known as the "dap." The odd greeting is a complicated series of handshakes and fist bumps that sometimes take several minutes. Among the black Marines in my unit, all pretty good friends of mine, I have never seen this done. Apparently these rear-area types are the only ones who have the time and/or inclination to perform this little sideshow. It is perhaps one of the strangest, most absurd, and silliest things I have ever seen ... thus far.

At the Post Exchange I buy a few civilian shirts, pants and a pair of shoes to wear in Singapore. All my personal gear and clothes have been stored in Okinawa. My buddy Riles, who not long ago returned from R&R in Hong Kong, advises me not to spend too much money on clothes. "You will need all your money," he says, smiling lecherously, "for more important things."

A commercial flight, complete with round-eyed female flight attendants (then called stewardesses) serve us an excellent meal and smile a lot. They are all extremely nice, smell good, and are treated with a certain amount of awe. However, no liquor is served. I suppose they most likely had problems with this in the past. It doesn't matter, as the perfume of these pretty young women is intoxicating enough.

Getting off the plane in Singapore it is like walking into a steam bath. The humidity is difficult to even describe. The northern provinces of South Vietnam are hot, but nothing to compare to this. It is akin to breathing water. Asian hostesses, smiling broadly and all quite stunning, meet us at the bottom of the aircraft steps and hand each of us a little frozen towel to wipe our faces. I am thinking this might, in the then current slang vernacular of the Marines, develop into something "decent."

I am nearly overcome with a sense of unreality. This whole thing, I conclude on the way to a luxury hotel, is nice but the experience is really bizarre. It is culture shock in reverse. The contrast and unfamiliar surroundings are making me a little dizzy and uncomfortable. Still I have every confidence I can rally and recover.

Two days ago I was sleeping in a hole in the ground, eating out of a can, and subsequently shitting openly in half of a nearby fifty-five gallon drum.

36

MISS CONGENIALITY

"If they didn't want to know, they shouldn't have asked."—James Webb

At the R&R center in Singapore a fat guy with a British accent and a safari shirt gives the assembled G.I.'s (Army, Air Force, Navy and Marines) the rules for the next five days. No drugs. No fighting. Try to buddy up with someone. Stay only in the approved hotels. If you end up in jail we may or may not be able to get you out. Singapore authorities do not put up with any foolishness. (Years later I read that an American teenager is "caned" in Singapore for an act of vandalism, despite all the efforts of the State Department to get a reprieve. This may be the reason the streets and sidewalks are so clean. Anyone caught littering is potentially whacked on the peepee ... or worse.)

Anyway, I get on one of the buses marked Sheraton. On it I meet Rick, a Marine sergeant stationed in Da Nang who works in supply and admits he has "a pretty good skate job. I have already extended three times. I'd rather be here than put up with some chickenshit duty back in the States." He seems like a pretty reasonable guy and we decide to partner up for the next five days or so.

At the Sheraton the "hostesses" are lined up for our inspection. It reminds me of a beauty contest, the only difference being we can go home with the contestant of our choice. I pick Miss Congeniality, a Chinese girl with flowing jet-black hair below her waist and a winning, friendly smile. Rick chooses a Malaysian girl with too much makeup and a haughty attitude. They both have American first names that coincide with the "girlfriend" fantasy in which we are all willing and eager participants. The mama-san in charge takes our money and advises that if for any reason either of the girls is unsatisfactory, we can trade them in the next morning. Kind of like buying an automobile and taking it on a test drive. (This whole

131

experience is fast approaching a level that is several degrees above bizarre.) And up to this point I am thoroughly enjoying the ride.

The first evening we spend in the hotel lounge eating, drinking and dancing to sixties music on a jukebox. The Exciters belt out "I Know Something About Love" while an inebriated Marine does a dance he calls the Cockroach. On his back on the dance floor, he wiggles and vibrates around like a giant dying bug. We laugh like complete idiots—perhaps just a little too hard. The girls seem to enjoy themselves even though I doubt any of them know "something about love." However, they certainly know a lot about lust. And a lot about horny nineteen-year-old kids on a five-day holiday from war.

My companion, whose American name I have forgotten and is made up anyway, does not speak very good English, but it is passable. Like the song says, "We never did too much talking anyway." Extremely clean, she complains that I am "dirty." What? Dirty? I took a cold-water shower just two days ago in Da Nang. The first one in over two months. Even used deodorant. She buys some kind of special soap and scrubs me down for over an hour. Once the red clay dirt is gone I am as white as an Easter lily. She still complains that I don't wash my hands enough. Out of the hand-washing habit, I start to explain the "why," but eventually give up. How do you explain that you have been living like a groundhog in a hole the last nine months?

Rick's girl is more interested in applying her makeup than partying. Also, apparently there is some kind of rift between the Chinese and Malaysians—some kind of racial thing which I never knew existed. There are a couple of heated exchanges between the two girls (although it is in Chinese, the anger comes through) and my "girlfriend" takes me aside.

"You ask your friend to get different girl," she says. "My girlfriend more fun. He like her beaucoup better. You ask, okay?" Okay, I say. What the hell.

The next morning the Malaysian girl is gone and a new girl arrives. Suzy. She speaks fluent English and is a delightful little fireball, telling stories, little jokes, and she knows her way around Singapore. She reminds me of the heroine in "The World of Suzie Wong." Rick says she has quite a number of other talents as well. It is a good trade.

We make a foursome and tour Singapore. Tiger Balm Gardens. Raffles Village. A fancy dinner at an upscale hotel. The movie "Bullitt" with Steve McQueen. Exhausted, I sleep through the whole thing. We also see a

Chinese "Kung Fu" movie, in Chinese, before this particular genre became wildly popular in the United States. (No doubt the most ridiculous thing I have ever seen.) I buy a Nikon camera and a little portable tape player. After three days I give the rest of my money to Miss Congeniality and tell her to make sure we have a good time. Since I am scheduled to return to Da Nang in a couple of days, the money will soon be virtually useless when I return to another isolated jungle outpost.

It is nice to be in the presence of a woman for a change. I have not even seen one in almost a year. Something about the softness and gentle feminine nature of a young woman is calming and extremely pleasant after months living in filth among men at war. At the Singapore Zoo we walk around holding hands. Although she is being paid and I harbor no illusions concerning the realities of this situation, she at least pretends to like me. I *know* I like her...

The night before I leave, my companion and tour guide takes me by her apartment. She lives there with her parents and her rambunctious little three-year-old girl. The kid is as cute as a speckled pup and watching her I am somewhat fascinated by her childish little antics. I had all but forgotten that innocence still exists. There are still kids in the world who giggle and play and take immense delight in the smallest of things. It seems strange ... and is an unexpected and hopeful little surprise.

Everyone is cordial but the little girl is standoffish as it comes time to leave. It is explained that "she doesn't like goodbyes." The girlfriend fantasy then begins to die in earnest. This whole experience, I realize suddenly, is nothing more than a simple business arrangement. There will be another lonely serviceman here next week taking my place. And the week after that, until Miss Congeniality gets too old and worn-out, or this insane war finally ends.

In retrospect, the sex is passionless, mechanical and mostly impersonal. It seems to be kind of mandatory in a strange way ... a validation of sorts that, for the time being at least, I am still alive. Actually, I don't remember much about the sexual activities, other than it being definitely better than nothing. A lot better.

I keep my paid companion's picture for many years. When I get married some ten years after the war, I finally throw the picture away. It does not seem appropriate to keep a photograph of a prostitute in the same box with wedding and family photographs.

But I do keep a picture of her little girl. Still.

37

DOGPATCH

"No one ever comes back from Vietnam. Not really."—Gary D. Schmidt

Dogpatch. The appropriate name of a dismal and pathetic collection of shacks of scrap lumber and tin just outside of Da Nang. It is a place, the Marines say, where you can get anything you want, from getting your throat slit to a terminal case of the clap. And everything in between. Like most villages near a military base, it is the territory of thieves, contraband, whores, con artists, black marketers, money changers, dope dealers, and AWOL servicemen. In other words, it is an extremely popular place most Marines want to frequent at every opportunity.

American military outposts sometimes have a tendency to morph nearby communities into something vile, bizarre and unrecognizable. It is a talent we Americans have honed to perfection over the last several wars. The whole island of Okinawa, for example, at least since the Vietnam debacle, has developed rather rapidly into one big combination floating bar and whorehouse. No wonder the Japanese hate us and want us to leave their island.

The plane ride back from Singapore a day earlier is quiet and in sharp contrast to the festive atmosphere of the R&R trip there a few days ago. Even the round-eyed stewardesses do little to elevate our dark and reflective moods. Any naive illusions relative to the war have been effectively shattered in the previous months, especially for those humping daily in the sweltering and oppressive heat and humidity that is the hallmark of Southeast Asia. Many of the Marines are leaving "girlfriends" for the first time in their short lives. For some, especially grunts returning to their line units, it will also be the last.

There are many stories of Marines killed in action a few days before their tour is complete and they are scheduled to "rotate" home. It happens.

37. Dogpatch

For those nearing the end of their respective combat tours, this is a frequently discussed possibility. As a result, "short-timers" are sometimes mercifully sent to the rear a couple of weeks before catching the "freedom bird" back to the Land of the Big PX. (Also known as "the World.") The consensus among the Marines is that if you are going to be killed, it is far better for it to happen the first week, rather than the last. Then, in common Marine logic, "you won't have to go through all this shit for nothing."

Rick, my supply sergeant R&R partner, wants to give me a guided tour of Dogpatch. I am spending the night in his rather comfortable hooch prior to flying back to my battalion headquarters in the morning. After the sterile streets of Singapore, the squalid contrast is striking. Dogpatch looks like a place where nothing good can possibly happen. And it doesn't. Much like—as I have learned the last nine months—most of the rest of Vietnam. I decline the invitation, as I have already seen enough of Dogpatch for one lifetime.

"Come on," Rick pleads, "I know some women there." Rick has been in Da Nang a few years and even speaks a little Vietnamese. Dogpatch is like a comfortable second home to him. It is interesting and amazing how people can so easily adapt to almost any environment ... even a Third World trash-pit village.

"Women?" I ask. "You mean whores?"

Rick shrugs and doesn't answer, which is an answer in itself. I reluctantly agree to go, although I am pretty confident we are not going to socialize with any Vietnamese princesses. Daisy Mae, the voluptuous sexpot in "Li'l Abner," I am reasonably certain does not reside in this particular Dogpatch.

Dogpatch looks and smells even worse the closer you get. We carry no weapons and I am uneasy around all these South Vietnamese. They look just like the North Vietnamese. There is a pervasive smell of raw sewage as well as rotten fish sauce, called *nuoc mam,* that the Vietnamese drench over most everything they eat. Unlike us highly civilized Americans, the Vietnamese do not burn their shit, but use it as fertilizer on the nearby rice paddies. The smell of burning shit, I arrogantly decide, is superior and preferable to this disgusting Vietnamese custom.

Now inside one of the dirt-floor hovels, Rick soon becomes involved in some sort of argument with a Vietnamese woman. Most of it is in Vietnamese and I don't know what it is about—nor care. A young girl, fifteen or sixteen years old and very pregnant, smiles at me seductively. This is one moral line, I immediately decide, that I have no intention of crossing, even though my personal lines have become increasingly blurry the last several months. This whole "tour," I conclude sadly, is a monumental bad idea. As I am trying to determine a way out, there is a furious knocking at what passes for a front door, followed by some frantic scurrying about, yelling, and apparent panic by the Vietnamese women inside the shack.

It is the White Mice. Corrupt and incompetent Vietnamese police in white uniforms, hence the derogatory name. Rick and I run out the back, not waiting around to find out what they want. I regret ever agreeing to this excursion, and blame myself for letting Rick talk me into coming in the first place. Getting shot in the back by White Mice in a shithole gook whorehouse does not correspond with my sometimes ridiculous fantasy of dying a war hero's gallant death. I resolve to be much more careful in the future.

Now it is way past curfew and back at the fenced compound the Marine guard will not let us in. "A Marine on guard duty has no friends." Rick knows the Marine and begins to beg him not to call the officer of the day. If he does, there will be trouble. How much I don't know, but I surmise this will not be a minor offense. Strangely enough, I am unconcerned and really could care less about any potential punishment. What can they do? Send me to Vietnam? Actually Rick, as a sergeant and NCO, would be in a lot more trouble than me anyway. Rank, as they say, has its privileges, but also a higher level of accountability. As a lowly lance corporal, if it comes to formal charges, I plan to play stupid. In this particular instance, it will not be an act.

The guard eventually relents and opens the gate for us. The next morning, I catch a flight back up north to my unit's headquarters at Quang Tri. Gone just seven days, nothing has changed ... except me.

Singapore already seems like a hazy but very pleasant dream.

HEATHEN KILLER

The new chevrons and Silver Star,
Pinned on by the battalion commander,
Are sweetened with a week of R&R.
A big mistake, we smirk,
And are rewarded with stories
Of an AWOL Chief
Busted
In a Hong Kong
Backstreet whorehouse,
By an unsuspecting cop.
Poor bastard...
Trying to rouse a sleeping Indian
From the Binge of the Century.
We celebrate Chief's return.
Walk to the LZ
Bearing gifts of canned fruit.
Beaming, he embraces us all.
A little thinner from a red line
Bread-and-water brig.
"Still a slick-sleeved private,"
He brags.
The officers shake their heads,
Go back to map reading,
And peer through binoculars.

38

A FROGMAN IN MIAMI

"My dad once told me his biggest challenge after returning from Vietnam had been coming to terms with his own callousness. He had made a deal with the war and traded his humanity for a ticket home."—Tucker Elliot

Back at Quang Tri headquarters after R&R nobody seems glad to see me. Not that I am the least bit surprised. None of these REMF's is a friend of mine and they are too busy putting in their time doing whatever REMF's do before the Slop Chute (enlisted club and beer hall) opens that evening. I plan to stay out of sight a day or two before heading back up to wherever my guys are now.

"Jones," I hear someone say. Looking around I see the voice belongs to a pipsqueak little administration sergeant who is the first sergeant's flunky and lapdog. A petty bureaucrat, he has an air of self-importance that is almost humorous—if it was not so irritating. I dislike the guy immensely and wish he would be sent up to the battery, where the real Marines would jerk a knot in his pompous ass. But it is not to be.

"Draw your gear from supply," Sgt. Pipsqueak says. "You have guard duty tonight on the perimeter."

Shit! These REMF's are always looking for somebody else to do their jobs. I protest vehemently, saying I need to get back to my unit, I just came back from R&R, my glasses are broke, and I think I caught something dangerous and highly contagious in Singapore. All efforts are to no avail.

It is three a.m. and I am sitting in a lawn chair (a benefit of guard duty in the rear) with an M-16 across my lap, staring into the darkness. The only way a gook would try to come through the wire here is if he somehow heard about the abundantly flowing beer and ice cream. It is an understatement to say it is difficult to keep my eyes open. Two other

139

Marines (FNG's) are in the bunker below me and we are taking two-hour shifts.

Footsteps crunch behind me and I turn around. It is a first lieutenant, the officer of the day, out checking the lines. Glad I wasn't asleep. Even if it is the rear, sleeping on guard duty can get you in a world of deep doo-doo. As it probably should.

"Were you sleeping, Marine?" he asks.

"No, Sir!" I reply, feigning shock at the mere suggestion. This is not a lie, but it is not exactly the truth either. Although I was not sleeping, neither was I awake; I was in that pleasant never-never land between the two extremes. My dream Chinese girlfriend was in the process of feeding me some delicious chicken with a pair of chopsticks before the lieutenant so rudely interrupted. Actually, the daydream had been reality just two days ago.

"Well," the "L.T." says, "you need to stay alert. A gook could slip in here and slit your throat." Only, I think, if he hears rumors about the doughnuts the chow hall makes every other day and wants to check it out for himself. But soon the lieutenant goes on down the line and I go back to my chopsticks-and-chicken fantasy. A good part is coming up next...

There is some movement just outside the concertina wire. I think. Maybe. Heart pounding, I am now wide awake. It is easy to turn shadows into suicide gook sappers and to let your imagination develop bogeymen out of trees and bushes. It's probably nothing. This is the rear, for God's sake, and they are probably making doughnuts at the chow hall right this very instant.

I am reminded of a story my dad told me about an incident that happened to him during the first days of World War II. Dropping out of high school right after Pearl Harbor and joining the military, Dad is sent to basic training at Miami Beach. The Army has taken over several of the high-rise luxury hotels to house trainees for the upcoming Main Event. On guard duty late one night, armed with an unloaded M-1 rifle, Dad sees a figure emerge from the surf and start walking toward the beach. "I thought I was dreaming," Dad says. "It's a frogman!" (Later, it is learned that German submarines stationed off our coast sometimes sent men into the United States for intelligence, sabotage and supply purposes.)

"Anyway," Dad continues, "I challenge him and he takes off running. I am gaining on him when he kicks off those swim fins and then really takes off. No way I can catch him now. So I call for the sergeant of the guard."

"You saw what?" the sergeant asks, amused. (These Kentucky hillbillies, he no doubt thinks of my father, can really come up with some weird-ass bullshit.) Chuckling to himself, the sergeant and the corporal of the guard walk up towards where Dad last saw the "frogman." They quit laughing when they find the flippers.

Now I am still looking intently just past the concertina wire. More movement. I am sure of it now. There is the beginning of the old fear and semi-panic. What a fool I am! Helmet, flak jacket, ammo and frags are down in the bunker with two sleeping FNG's. Here I am sitting in a lawn chair thinking about fucking doughnuts. I am so unbelievably stupid I deserve to get myself killed.

Someone in a bunker to my left sets off a pop-up flare. They see something too. So this is definitely not just my overactive imagination. The flare hisses and pops and floods the whole area in a ghostly white magnesium light. I can see the figure clearly now, threading carefully through the wire...

It is a mongoose.

39

A LOT OF FAT SAILORS

"In war the heroes always outnumber the soldiers ten to one."—H. L. Mencken

At Quang Tri, the morning after my epic and dangerous encounter with the mongoose, Sgt. Pipsqueak calls me aside. I am reasonably certain he despises me, and consequently I know this encounter will be an unpleasant one. Perhaps he can sense I think he is an arrogant, incompetent, noncombatant, REMF, chickenshit pogue and fool. Also, I resent the fact that even though he is all these things, he has complete and total power over my immediate future. As a sergeant, he is holding all the cards, whereas my hand is more or less a total bust.

"I am going to send you to get your glasses fixed before you go back out," he says.

Well ... maybe I have misjudged the guy. Perhaps he is looking out for me. But I am still suspicious. A zebra cannot change its stripes and Sgt. Pipsqueak thinks his stripes make him God of the Universe. An ulterior motive will no doubt surface soon enough.

At the Battalion Aid Station, I board a chopper headed for a hospital ship in the South China Sea, the USS *Repose*. Perhaps this *may* turn out to be decent. I can get lost for a couple days on the ship and also eat myself into a stupor on some good Navy chow. Navy personnel always eat better than anyone else. There are a lot of fat sailors.

The USS *Repose* is a big white ship with a Red Cross on its side that steams back and forth along the coast of South Vietnam. A modern floating hospital, its crew treats the endless stream of casualties flowing in from Vietnam. In 1969, there are a lot of them. The medevac choppers land frequently, every few minutes or so, unloading mostly half-dead grunts. Many of them are so filthy you cannot tell if they are black or white. Not that it makes any difference.

142

39. A Lot of Fat Sailors

On first glimpse the gleaming white hospital ship reminds me of a luxury cruise liner. But there are some major differences. No pool. No alcohol. No shuffleboard games or casino. And all these passengers are in some degree or another of fucked-upness. I do not see any women on the ship, but the rumor is that some American Red Cross girls working onboard will play the "hokey-pokey" for enough money. A story circulates that one girl went home after six months with over fifty thousand dollars—a huge sum in 1969. But I never see any Red Cross girls. Perhaps it is all some sex-starved Marine's fantasy.

After a lens in my glasses is replaced, I eat lunch in the ship's mess hall. Unbelievable! Fried chicken, fresh milk, bread, an array of desserts. I eat so much I think I may throw up. It may be worth getting wounded just for the ... well, maybe not.

The choppers are still arriving with their damaged and dying cargo and the scene is getting a little depressing. In addition, the hallways of the ship are full of little Vietnamese children, many with missing arms and/or legs, scooting, hopping and crawling along the decks. They are the happiest kids I have ever seen—smiling, laughing, trying to engage you in some way or another. I suppose the hospital ship is a paradise compared to whatever miserable situation got them here in the first place. For some reason, I find this equally depressing. Things are simply not working out as I had planned. Do they ever?

There is another thing making me a little uncomfortable. The ship is almost entirely populated with very sick people, damaged kids, or Marines with catastrophic, life-changing battle injuries. And here I am strolling through the ship's passages with a pair of broken glasses. That afternoon, I catch the first available chopper back to Quang Tri.

Sgt. Pipsqueak is in the battalion office when I return. The smirking, self-important little asshole tells me to report to him first thing in the morning. "Got some news for you," he adds, with his customary smirk. I am sure he could tell me now, but that would deprive him of the pleasure of letting me think about it all night. Only three months to go. I am getting weary of all this rear-area pogue foolishness. Once I get back to my unit, among friends, things will be infinitely better.

That evening I go to the Slop Chute and drink too many fifteen-cent beers. Later, the night is full of dreams about Sgt. Pipsqueak. In one, I am beating him mercilessly with a large stick used to stir burning barrels of shit.

40

THINGS ARE DIFFERENT OUT THERE

"The only thing that makes battle psychologically tolerable is the brother-hood among soldiers. You need each other to get by."—Sebastian Junger

"I have trouble with direction because I have trouble with authority. I was not a good Marine."—Gene Hackman

At the morning formation in Quang Tri after returning from the hospital ship 1st Sgt. Bulldog is not present. Sgt. Pipsqueak is in charge. He struts and postures before the little group of Marines, basking in the glory of his temporary authority. The show is preposterous but also highly amusing. I find myself smiling and recall Charlie Chaplin in the silent movie "The Great Dictator." But today I hope to return to my battery, away from this silliness, entertaining as it may be.

"See me in the office," Sgt. Pipsqueak says as we are dismissed. Hopefully, he will tell me I am leaving today. Either that or he caught a glimpse of me unsuccessfully trying to stifle a grin during his morning performance and has something "special" planned. I have a growing sense of foreboding and uneasiness as I approach the battalion office. Perhaps I should have been a little more respectful, kissed his ass a little. But this thought passes quickly as I think of my guys living like moles, struggling to stay alive on some remote jungle ghetto of a firebase. I can't wait to get back to them and relate my R&R adventures, my trip to the USS *Repose*, the ridiculous antics of these clean-shaven, spit-polished booted office pinkies and arrogant administrative NCO's. I will exaggerate the stories, adding my own little humorous observations, sprinkle in some bullshit, and have them all laughing and begging for more.

Sgt. Pipsqueak looks up from a stack of papers he is studying intently like it is a document just received to end the Vietnam War. Probably a requisition order for more bug repellant. The guy just brings out the worst in me. I can't seem to help myself.

"Jones," he says, smirking like an egg-sucking mongrel dog. "Got a hot news flash for you..."

This cannot be good. Too late for any ass kissing now. I don't reply and wait for the hammer to drop.

"You are *not* going back to the battery," he says after a suitable dramatic pause. Obviously he is enjoying himself immensely. I act like he just said, "Well, it may rain next week."

"Does this mean," I say offhandedly, "I can go home now?" It occurs to me, much too late, that my sarcastic attitude has not served me well. But at this point I guess it doesn't really matter. I can tell my seemingly cavalier attitude irritates the shit out of Sgt. Pipsqueak. Which, of course, is my intention all along...

"They need someone up at Alpha-Two," he says flatly. "And you are going."

My "I don't give a rat's ass" demeanor is really beginning to frustrate him now. His little pogue rodent face is starting to turn red. Maybe, I think, the game has now gone a little too far and I may have just defecated in my own rice bowl. But the cards are already dealt.

"Where is Alpha-Two?" I ask. I have never heard of the place, although I know instinctively that if he is sending me there, it has to be a "world-class" shithole.

"That," he says evenly, "is none of your goddamn business."

During the Vietnam War there are at least six hundred documented cases of American troops killing their own NCO's and officers in what were called "fragging" incidents. Another fourteen hundred are injured or killed under "mysterious" circumstances. If the military admits to *this* many, you can be sure there were considerably more as the brass tries to downplay these events and attempts to sweep these sad affairs under a very large rug. Curiously, most of these fraggings happen in the rear, non-combat, safe areas. Mostly with U.S. Army units. I never heard of it with any of the Marine units I served with, but that doesn't mean it never happened. As one U.S. congressman said during hearings as the American Army in Vietnam was imploding and virtually out of control during the early 1970s: "Second lieutenants have been shot in the back for a thousand years..."

Strangely enough, Sgt. Pipsqueak's answer does not make me the least bit angry. I certainly have no desire to roll a grenade under his bunk, although no one (NCO's or officers) in my unit ever talked to me in the manner Sgt. Pipsqueak does. Things are much different out there. In retrospect, Sgt. Pipsqueak is merely feeling guilty and inferior for his comfortable and soft life in the rear. Which I would assume for REMF's is most likely a common and fairly widespread condition. But they are what they are, and it is all the luck of the draw anyway. In any war there is enough guilt to go around. But I would not trade places with Sgt. Pipsqueak, or anyone else here at battalion headquarters for that matter, even if it were possible.

Later that morning, I gather my gear and load my "just-three-months-to-go" young ass aboard a northbound truck convoy to Alpha-2. Wherever the hell it is. I guess I will find out soon enough. Hopefully, my next trip to the rear will be on the way home. Maybe this new place won't be so bad. It doesn't hurt to think positive.

With just one exception, I never see any of my guys at the battery again.

41

SEARCH AND AVOID

*"Now we can see clearly, like light at the end of a tunnel."—General
Henri Navarre, French Forces, Vietnam*

A couple days at Alpha-2 and I come to a realization that I have suspected all along. The war is lost. The United States will never prevail in
this part of Southeast Asia and it is foolish to even consider otherwise.
The South Vietnamese do not care, have lost the will to fight (if in fact
they ever had it to begin with), the North Vietnamese are prepared to go
"all in" for as long as necessary, and the United States is "war weary" and
does not have the stomach or political will to continue. Unfortunately, we
will continue the charade for several more years. (Robert McNamara, secretary of Defense, wrote in his biography that he knew the war was
unwinnable early on, but said nothing while another thirty thousand
Americans were lost.)

Alpha-2, just outside a little village named Gio Linh, is a few hundred
yards south of the DMZ. To the east is the South China Sea. Due west is
a place called Con Thien (it translates to "Place of Angels" in Vietnamese)
that is the sight of another previously gallant and costly stand by the U.S.
Marines. Alpha-2 is the furthest northern allied position, manned by
approximately twelve Marines, a U.S. Army self-propelled eight-inch howitzer cannon and crew, a battery of six South Vietnamese Army 105 millimeter cannons, and an infantry company of the South Vietnamese Army
which provides security. At least they are supposed to be providing security. I have no confidence in these "little people" at all, as they seem to be
more interested in holding hands and smoking cigarettes than anything
else. When the North Vietnamese invade some four years later, Alpha-2
is the first position to be overrun. No surprise.

The Marines here man a sixty-five-foot-high observation tower and

View from observation tower at Alpha-2 into North Vietnam.

monitor the North Vietnamese on the other side of the river. We watch them through an oversized powerful pair of ship's binoculars and through a night-vision "Starlight" scope. Due to a bombing halt, declared by President Lyndon Johnson, we are not allowed to fire artillery across the Ben Hai River, which separates the two countries. The NVA knows this and has raised a huge red flag just on the other side of the river, moving troops around at will in the open, and at night infiltrating people and supplies across the river under the cover of darkness. It is maddening. The NVA is symbolically dropping its trousers and giving us a fuck-you "moon shot," and there is nothing we can do.

Most late afternoons Vietnamese peasant women, clad in black pajamas, straw cone hats, and carrying long poles with baskets on the ends, do that bouncy little running walk they do en route to a large group of trees a few hundred yards west of us. They are either taking supplies to an NVA mortar crew or providing cover for them. The mortars usually fall on us just before dark. We are subsequently never given clearance to return fire into the trees, as headquarters says there are "friendlies" in the area. Apparently the friendlies are these very same women. Although they don't seem all that friendly to me ... especially when they start dropping in mortar rounds on a regular basis. If we ever do get clearance to fire, the NVA will be long gone by then.

One afternoon as I am working the tower I spot a gook running toward the trees from a position to the west not too far from us. He doesn't appear to have a weapon, but he is most certainly a spotter for the NVA mortars. There is simply no other reason for him to be there. A small fixed-winged aircraft called a Bird Dog is patrolling the DMZ and I get the pilot on the radio. If I can get a halfway good location on this spotter gook, I can call in some pulverizing artillery and ruin his whole day.

"I'll go down and take a look," the pilot says. These guys are flying unarmed in slow-flying aircraft and usually call the shots for artillery and airstrikes. They have a massive overdose of testosterone—with a capital T. I see this one swoop down low over the trees. "I don't see him," he says.

"He is right in that tree line, Sir," I reply. (All pilots are officers, hence the "Sir.") I am getting frustrated. This is a chance for a little payback and the running gook is definitely in there ... somewhere. I saw him just a minute ago. If I can just determine his general area, even within a couple hundred yards, I will call in enough artillery high-explosive firepower around him that even a cockroach will not survive.

"I don't even see the tree line," the pilot reports.

I don't know what to say. This is an unbelievable turn of events. Don't see the tree line? "What do you mean ... Sir?" I ask. This war is getting increasingly more bizarre. I wonder why I continue to even try.

"I know it probably looks like a tree line from where you are," the pilot says, sensing my disgust. "But it's really not a tree line, just a bunch of vegetation with some scattered trees. But don't sweat it. We will get him another day."

It is certainly not the pilot's fault. Nothing, I think, is ever what it seems in this strange and mystery-shrouded country. The surrounding jungle, along with the bitter truth of this crazy war, is so often just an allusive and deceptive apparition. You might say this entire place is kind of getting on my nerves.

The next day from the tower I watch a platoon of the South Vietnamese Army leave the perimeter on a search-and-destroy patrol. As is their custom, they go behind a little hill, sit there all day smoking, eating and shooting the shit, then straggle casually back into our outpost in the afternoon. They have absolutely no desire to engage the enemy. But then again, especially here lately, neither do I. We immediately reclassify these phony sham patrols as "search and avoid." Another example of how our efforts over the years in Vietnam have developed steadily into a pointless and ultimately fatal exercise in futility. Nevertheless, our political elite continue to furiously and shamelessly beat a dead horse—a decaying horse that is perhaps a symbol of the Vietnam War itself.

In fact, this particular horse has already been dead for so long, it is now thoroughly rotten and really starting to stink.

42

GO ALONG TO GET ALONG

"There must be some way outta here
Said the joker to the thief
There is too much confusion
I can't get no relief."
                            —Jimi Hendrix

"Hell no, we won't go."—Vietnam antiwar slogan

Alpha-2 is getting a new lieutenant to manage the twelve Marines assigned here. Previously, the highest ranking man is a sergeant E-5. But apparently the high muckety-muck authorities back in Quang Tri decide we need more and closer supervision. Plus, all these new lieutenants are going to need some sort of job. Not such a bad idea, really. In the rear there are simply too many chiefs supervising too few Indians. And it must be remembered that all God's second lieutenants must get their combat arms "ticket" punched per Marine Corps policy and custom.

Some of the younger officers are shocked to discover that the same rules of enlisted/officer relationships prevalent in the peace-time Marines Corps do not apply in combat zones. The same military courtesies exist, but not necessarily to the same degree as back at camps Lejeune and Pendleton. It takes a certain amount of adjustment for these lieutenants, not long out of Basic School, to realize they are still a "sir," but on a probationary status until they prove themselves. Exceptions abound but this is generally how it works. And it works pretty well.

My job, for example, as an artillery forward observer on the DMZ, is usually the billet of an officer—or at least a staff NCO. I am just a lowly lance corporal, two stripes above a private, but I have the authority to fire tens of thousands of dollars' worth of artillery at any real or imagined targets I so choose. (If I can get clearance.) I never see any higher-ups in the tower, with the lone exception of our new lieutenant, who will occasionally climb up to chew my ass about some little thing or another in an effort to assert and/or establish his authority. This may be a little unfair because it does not happen more than once … or twice at the most. (And I can't even remember what it was about.) Nevertheless, I always respond with "Yes, Sir," or "No, Sir" to whatever chickenshit thing it is, or "It won't happen again, Sir." This always seems to work with him and I consequently never have any trouble getting along—with this officer anyway. "Go along to get along" is my new and improved motto and strategy. A little respect for the lieutenant's real and perceived authority, along with some light ass-kissing techniques work wonders to keep him happy, off my case, and, much more importantly, out of the tower.

The new lieutenant is a nice enough guy, but he is inexperienced and understandably a little unsure of himself in his new position. After quietly observing things for a few days he comes up to me with a suggestion. Which, coming from an officer, is basically the same as a direct order.

"I notice when you pull your shift in the tower you don't take your weapon," he begins. "If we are attacked you could return fire from the tower." This is not a good idea but by now I know better than to argue. That type of mindless strategy, employed most recently with Sgt. Pipsqueak, is what got me here in the first fucking place. The tower, sticking up like a giant erect penis sixty-five feet in the air, has no protection from small arms fire. Secondly, in any ground attack the tower is a high value target for the gooks, since we are the "eyes of arty [artillery]" and can bring considerable fire and destruction upon their rotten-fish-sauce-eating little heads. If the gooks get that close, my best option will be on the ground where I will have some semblance of cover and at least a fighting chance. And that is exactly where I will be…

"Yes, Sir!" I reply enthusiastically. "I never thought of that." (It takes me awhile, but eventually I learn.) I don't know if there is another shithole worse than this one, but with less than ninety days to go on my thirteen-month tour I am not taking any chances. The lieutenant beams with satisfaction and walks away. The poor guy wants to feel relevant, like he is doing something important. It's kind of sad, really. I take my weapon with me for a few days and then forget about it. It is too difficult to carry up the sixty-five-foot ladder and if there is a ground attack I am not staying up there anyway. The lieutenant's ill-conceived but good-intentioned and "brilliant" idea is never mentioned again.

This small outpost called Alpha-2 is established from the remnants

42. Go Along to Get Along

of a small base the French built years ago before their infamous defeat at Dien Bien Phu. Our new lieutenant, along with me and five other Marines, reside in one of the old bunkers. Another six Marines are housed in yet another bunker a short distance away. I have not a single clue as to the primary function—or any function for that matter—of these other Marines or even the nature of their jobs. Seldom do they come up to the tower. Communications maybe, or some kind of intelligence gathering. Who knows?

What I do know is that they have turned their bunker into a psychedelic party house and marijuana emporium. Perpetually burning incense has the place smelling like a Vietnamese whorehouse. Decorated with colorful orange-and-white parachutes hanging from the ceiling, a great sound system blasts Jimi Hendrix's "All Along the Watchtower" and Grace Slick of the Jefferson Airplane's "White Rabbit." They even have an ornate "Turkish water pipe" to smoke what they proudly classify as the best pot God ever created. It is rumored they occasionally smuggle young girls up from Gio Linh to spend the night. After a while they invite me over, but I respectfully decline. The dope smoking does not appeal to me and I have little interest in anything (up to and including the clap) the local whores have to offer.

A sergeant is supposedly in charge of this head shop and doper haven, but he is also the chief pothead. And he seems to have a lot of authority. Our new lieutenant catches one of the guys from Chief Pothead's bunker smoking dope and has him locked up in a metal Conex box awaiting transfer to the rear the next day. Chief Pothead has him released, although the offending Marine does indeed leave the following day, allegedly to face charges. That night the party in the bunker continues unabated. Nothing changes.

Late one afternoon, just about dusk, I am in the tower pulling my regular shift. Several Marines from the infamous dope palace are lounging on top of their bunker. Mortars begin to fall and they scramble inside for safety. All except one Marine, now prone and seriously hit. The first mortar round gets him. Marines pour back out of the bunker and drag the wounded guy back inside. They may be dopers, but they are still Marines and they take care of their own. Having just been relieved, I go down to see if I can be of any help. Somebody else can deal with trying—unsuccessfully I am almost certain—to return fire on the offending enemy mortars.

153

The Body Burning Detail

A Marine, coincidentally named Mac like my former partner, is lying on the bunker floor being treated by a seemingly competent Army medic from the big eight-inch artillery howitzer nearby. Mac is still conscious but his color looks bad. It appears that shrapnel has struck him in the chest. Rapidly taking short breaths, he is very frightened.

"I can't breathe, Doc," Mac is whispering, "I can't breathe."

"Relax, Mac ... relax," the medic says. "This is normal. Medevac is on the way."

It doesn't seem very normal to me. Or apparently to the medic either. He turns and tells someone behind him, low enough so Mac can't hear, to rush up the medevac chopper. Mac is turning gray and I am thinking this is just one more Mac who won't make it home. A chopper is thumping faintly in the distance. This is not a regular medevac helicopter, but a nearby twin-rotor Marine chopper that hears the urgent call and decides to respond. The chopper crew must know that once they get here the gooks will let loose with another mortar barrage in an effort to win the coveted "Gook Helicopter Medal." The chopper still comes, mortars be damned. (Where, I think, do they find these guys?)

"When the bird gets close," the medic is saying, "you guys grab a corner and let's get him out there."

I am getting much too "short" for this bullshit, but end up with a corner of the litter anyway. We run with the stretcher to the landing helicopter as a mortar round explodes a few yards away. The gooks are trying to bracket the chopper, with some success, and more rounds are on the way. A thought comes to me. It is "Sweet Jesus, bless us sinners now and in the hour of our death...." I have no idea whence this comes. I am not even Catholic. The old fear has once again surfaced with a vengeance—but not nearly as bad as before. It is as if, with almost a year here, I have reached a point somewhere past caring. Strange, in a way, but true enough. Another mortar explodes right behind the landing zone as the gooks continue to zero us in. Nevertheless, we get to the chopper unscathed as the back ramp comes down.

Some South Vietnamese Army soldiers have also been wounded and are trying to get aboard. They have one guy in a poncho and we jostle for position at the ramp's edge. The guy is obviously already dead, eyes open and teeth full of blood, and I resent the fact they are trying to get him on the chopper before our live guy. He is, after all, just another dead gook. The gunners help everyone on board and within seconds the chopper lifts off and is gone. I don't sleep much that night. The face of the dead South Vietnamese soldier, eyes still open, and with a gruesome bloody death grin, keeps surfacing in my dreams.

A couple days later while I am in the tower a Huey lands and several officers get out and come to the base of the tower. "Can we come up?" one yells.

"Sure!" I yell back. "Come on up." (As if I had a choice...)

They look through the big ship's binoculars at the huge NVA flag flying across the river. The big red flag with a yellow star has become somewhat of a tourist attraction. Having now actually seen the object of their curiosity, they can now make a hasty exit back to the officer's club in Da Nang and tell everyone they have been up to the DMZ. Maybe write themselves up for a medal or two. One of the officers, a colonel, seems approachable and I start to ask him if he knows that the war is lost. Surely, he knows. At this stage of the game, almost everyone knows. But I decide against it, as his answer will not change anything and whatever his reply, it will not make one iota of difference. I do ask him about Mac, the Marine seriously wounded just a few days before. Can he find out his status for me?

"Oh, I'm sure he will be just fine," the colonel says. After about ten minutes they load back up into their Huey and quickly fly away.

43

FIRE ANTS
ON A DEAD BIRD

"This is one crazy white-man's war."—Chief, Hopi Marine

The lieutenant tells me to come along with him as he analyzes impact areas in order to determine the location of the NVA mortar crew that just wounded the second Mac. (Or possibly killed him, as I never did find out if he survived.) We measure angles and dig holes, although even a retarded rock ape could figure out the origin of these incoming mortars. I want to scream and point—they're right over there! This seems like a complete waste of time, but in keeping with my nonsmart-ass cooperative attitude I assist the new lieutenant with fervor and enthusiasm. Although slightly ashamed for not speaking my mind, we "short-timers" do what we have to do.

One of the mortar rounds has gone through the tin roof of the South Vietnamese Army's mess area and landed in the middle of a table. They were eating at the time and I suppose this is where the South Vietnamese soldier who was loaded in the chopper was killed. There are still bowls of half-eaten rice on the table, some of which contain bloody chunks of human flesh. Even though I saw many things even more horrific than this, for some reason this bizarre image stays with me all these years.

Once a week we load up a big truck and take the outpost's garbage to a dump on the outskirts of Gio Linh. A lot of Vietnamese live at the trash pit, wretched and desperate-looking people residing in makeshift cardboard-and-tin shelters. As soon as we arrive a swarm of kids descends upon us like fire ants on a dead bird, searching for scraps of food and anything they might be able to sell or trade. For some reason this has little effect on me, for at this point I am somewhat emotionally detached from

43. Fire Ants on a Dead Bird

Vietnamese orphans living at Gio Linh trash dump.

almost any form of death or suffering. The shrinks, I learn much later, call this "psychic numbing." Recalling the scene now, with my own child and grandkids, it affects me infinitely more than it ever did then.

At Alpha-2, for the first time I am interacting with the American Army, whose soldiers crew the big howitzer assigned to the outpost. Army soldiers are different from Marines. Much different ... although I find them to be good guys and extremely competent artillerymen. Many of them are draftees, more so than in the

Misery personified—young boy at trash dump.

157

The Body Burning Detail

Marines, and consequently they speak their minds and have little use for military protocol. They argue with the staff NCO's on a level that simply would not be tolerated in the Marine Corps. The junior officers are often just like "one of the guys." Although the Army has many excellent elite units, rank-and-file soldiers seem to lack the swagger and generally cocky and superior attitude common among Marines. At least that is my experience. From day one, Marines are force fed the idea that we are the finest and most efficient fighting force in the history of the world. (Whether or not this is accurate is open for debate.) The remarkable thing is that almost all Marines believe it to be true.

I never develop friendships with the Marines at Alpha-2 like those I know back in my battery. Maybe I am not there long enough. Or maybe we do not share enough good times ... or even not-so-good times. Perhaps, instinctively, I do not want to get that close to anyone else. But it is most probably because I now act like a convict serving hard time, counting down the days till my sentence is complete, looking and waiting for the day I finally walk out the prison gates, once again a free man.

One particularly unpleasant incident occurs at Alpha-2 among the Marines in my bunker. We always have more C-rations than we can eat, so I take several cases to the South Vietnamese Army battery and sell them for Vietnamese money called dong. The money is for sodas and/or anything else we might need and can buy from the local gooks. One Marine, a pogue up from Quang Tri, takes exception to this and claims I am "illegally disposing of government property." True enough, although at first I think he must surely be kidding. He most assuredly is not. An REMF germ has apparently infected his brain. Here we are a few hundred yards from potential annihilation, blowing up gooks and getting blown up by gooks, at least some of us smoking dope and consorting with whores, living day by day in dangerous, filthy and primitive conditions. But for God's sake, let us not cross into *illegal territory* and sell any of these foul and semi-edible C-rations!

We almost come to fisticuffs over it, but primarily because I refuse to engage him, we do not. Maybe I should have anyway. In the end, though, I decide it is not a cause worth making a stand over. Nothing here is. In fact, nothing in this entire godforsaken country is worth the bloodshed, misery and sacrifices I have seen thus far. Embittered? I am—more than just a little. Nevertheless, this latest petty sordid encounter leaves a bad taste in my mouth. I can't leave this place soon enough. I can't leave Vietnam soon enough. I have little more than a month to go.

A few days later our new lieutenant—who really is a pretty decent sort and, if he survives, will no doubt develop into a fine officer—meets me at the base of the tower as I come down from a shift. "Pack your trash," he says solemnly, "you are leaving in the morning."

Immediately I have a sudden sick and rapidly sinking feeling of dread. My new ass-kissing, model–Marine, super cooperative, I'm-happy-as-a-dead-pig-in-a-mud-hole-to-be-here strategy has failed miserably and it looks as if I am off to yet another infamous and detestable shithole. Maybe, I hope, this will be the last one.

"Where am I going now?" I ask, resigned once again to an uncertain but inevitable fate.

"Well," the lieutenant says, breaking into a huge grin, "you are going home."

It takes me a moment to realize the lieutenant has just been fucking with me. It is hard to believe. Going home. A month early!

Perhaps there is a God in heaven after all.

44

FULL CIRCLE

"No matter how cynical I get ... I just can't seem to keep up."—Lily Tomlin

At Alpha-2 we never get much beer. Actually, we never get any. Therefore I try to make up for the deficit the first night back in Quang Tri. The next morning I don't feel like getting up and going to formation. So I don't go.

Sgt. Pipsqueak shows up a little later at the transient's hooch where I am bunking. At first, I think he is there about my missing the formation. No such luck. Sgt. Pipsqueak is the elementary school hall monitor, drunk with power and "little man" phony confidence. How I ever got crossways with him is a mystery to me. Actually, it is not much of a mystery. I treat him like the little self-righteous prick that he is even though I know this is a battle I will not, cannot win.

"Jones," he begins smugly. "I have you assigned to burn the shitters this morning. You need to get up and get after it. They have not been burned for a few days and are nice and full by now." This is Sgt. Pipsqueak's finest hour and he is having difficulty containing his glee.

"Get somebody else," I say calmly. "I am not doing it. That is an FNG job. I am not an FNG. The answer is 'No Thanks.'"

Sgt. Pipsqueak looks like he has just been informed he has inoperable testicular cancer. "Are you refusing?" he sputters, red faced. "Are you refusing a direct order?" I think he is going to hyperventilate. This is absolutely the most fun I have had since R&R. Whatever happens next may even be worth it, although I have my doubts.

"We will see about this!" he announces in the most authoritative voice he can muster. "We will see what the first sergeant has to say about it." Sgt. Pipsqueak scurries away like the little tattletale rat he is. The hall monitor is going to tell the teacher.

44. Full Circle

Returning a few minutes later he has regained his composure and is as smirking and cocky as a young pimp on a street corner. "Top wants to see you," he says. "Right now."

Uh, oh. Sgt. Pipsqueak is an amusing cartoon character, but 1st Sgt. Bulldog ("Top") is the real deal. The game has just been notched up several levels. I will plead my case to Top, but I would be a total fool to cross him.

"Come on in, Jones," Top says from behind his desk at headquarters. "Sit down." Sgt. Pipsqueak is nowhere around. "How are you doing?" he continues. Top has always been civil to me. When someone actually has some real authority, unlike the Pipsqueak turd, he usually doesn't flaunt or abuse it.

"Pretty good, Top. Ready to go home. I have enjoyed about as much of this as I can stand."

Top smiles slightly at my little joke. A busy man, he then gets right down to it. "I hear," he says, "you are not going to burn the shitters?"

Then, with passion and conviction, I launch full force into my defense. "I burned the shitters when I first got here, burning shitters is an FNG job, I am a lance corporal now and no longer an FNG, some new private or PFC needs the experience, I have to get ready to rotate to the States." And so forth.

Top holds up his hand. "Enough," he says. "You don't have to burn the shitters if you don't want to."

"I don't?" I ask. "Well ... thanks, Top." I get up to leave.

"One more thing," Top adds. "I'm going to pull your orders for a flight date. When the South Vietnamese all go to the States, you will still be here."

A wise man always weighs his options. It does not take long to weigh mine. "Which way to the shitters, Top?"

I have come full circle. It's a fitting and glorious end to an illustrious and eventful tour in Southeast Asia. Burning shit in the beginning. A year later, still stirring burning barrels of shit.

But a lot of shit happens in between.

45

TIGER PISS

"I don't miss the circus ... but I do miss the clowns."—Anonymous

*"At the going down of the sun
And in the morning
We will remember them..."*
—Laurence Binyon, World War I poet

On Okinawa, en route back to the States, I pick up my stored gear and receive new uniforms. The old ones don't fit anymore. I am down to one hundred thirty pounds and eating any spicy or rich food makes me sick as a grass-eating dog. It takes years for my digestive system to get back to normal. They also give us a new ribbon, which was recently developed and I had never seen before. The Marine Corps now issues this ribbon to distinguish combat troops from pogues. It's like the Army's Combat Infantryman's Badge. I like this distinction although no one, pogue or otherwise, when it comes down to the nitty-gritty, has any influence on where they are initially assigned. It is all a crapshoot, really. No doubt Sgt. Pipsqueak, power-and-glory whore that he is, will manipulate the system to get one of these Combat Action Ribbons, even though his major combat experience primarily consists of trying to get someone (primarily me) to burn the shitters. I still dislike the guy...

One night in "Okie" I am out without a proper uniform, or even "liberty" permission, with other homebound Marines. We have imbibed more than our share of Tiger Piss, a Japanese beer in tall bottles that costs a dollar each and contains a little extra kick. The stuff is probably full of formaldehyde or some equally potent brain-cell-killing ingredient. Rather than trying to sneak back on base by climbing the fence, we stupidly decide this particular act would be far, far beneath our drunken dignity. We unanimously decide, after a short alcohol-fueled conference, to walk right through the main gate. What are they going to do? Send us to Vietnam? Been there. In sober retrospection this is a fantastically dumb and potentially "brig time" decision. Although they may not send us back to Vietnam, time in the Okinawa brig is a distinct possibility.

At the main gate one of the MP's looks like someone I think I recognize. It is three a.m. and we are loud, stupid and staggeringly jackass drunk. A closer look and I see it is my friend Rivera, the Marine who suffered the head wound at LZ Argonne. It is, as they say, blind and dumb shit-house luck. Rivera, now a military policeman on gate duty, hustles us inside before someone sees us and we get arrested. "You idiots," he says, "get your drunk asses in here." I suppose God really does take care of drunks and fools.

Sgt. Chase Jones, Weapons Platoon, 3rd Battalion, 3rd Marines, Iraq, 2007.

Our gear is searched in Okinawa for contraband, mostly weapons and dope, and the sergeant searching mine confiscates my prized NVA scalp. I protest long and loudly, without success. "You can't," he explains, somewhat wearily, "take body parts back to the civilized world." I had planned to hang it from the rearview mirror of my 1966 Mustang. I know this sounds sick and bizarre. It is without question barbaric, but such barbarity is one of the many bitter fruits and grotesque, unexplainable aftermaths and reality of any war. I offer no excuses.

From Okinawa I continue on to the Marine base at Twenty-nine Palms (aka Twenty-nine Stumps) in California. I am asked there if I want to reenlist or get an "early out." After leave and travel time, I have less than three months left of my two-year obligation. The Marines, for all

The Body Burning Detail

Leaving I Corps as helicopter gunner ruins the picture.

practical purposes, are through with me. And so I head home. My home-coming is kind of bittersweet, as in the similar experiences of all returning combat veterans. I am simply not the same dumbass kid who went to war. Home has not changed. The changes—from subtle to monumental and life altering—are all internal and invisible.

When I get there I find that no one wants to hear or talk about Viet-nam. Not even my own family. My dad (God rest his soul) says he'd rather not hear about what happened, or what I did over there. It makes me angry. What does he think I was doing? But I hold no resentment. It is his way and I suppose he rationalizes that he has worried and fretted enough about me. And I suppose he has. It is time to put Vietnam and the war in that rearview mirror and get on with life. Like tens of thousands of other veterans, I soon learn this is much easier said than done.

Applying for jobs, I find it is no asset to mention my status as a Viet-nam veteran. Americans are tired of the war, perhaps even a little ashamed. They want no reminders. In my hometown, some of my high school friends, now well into their college careers, see me and ask: "I haven't seen you around lately. Have you been somewhere?"

45. Tiger Piss

In writing this book, I tell my own son, a Marine infantry sergeant and combat veteran of Iraq and Afghanistan, that I have some misgivings that many may find this book disturbing, on a number of levels. (At times, *I* find the writing of it disturbing.) But he gives me some typical Marine-to-Marine advice: "Write the book, Dad," he says. "Tell it exactly like it was. And if they don't like it ... well, fuck 'em."

Several years after Vietnam I still have disturbing dreams and struggle with some depression. One dream, involving loading dead and dying Marines aboard helicopters, I may have had thousands of times. Every night or so for a long, long time...

I go to the Veterans Administration and someone sets me up with a shrink, who loads me up with antidepressants—a myriad of pills that I eventually quit taking. I prefer genuine depression rather than chemically induced flatness and false contentment. I see the psyche doctor once a week for at least a couple of years. I like the guy and tell him everything I can remember: about both Macs and the twenty-two Marines KIA at LZ Argonne and the rice bowls with human flesh and Hutch and the burning gooks and Sgt. Pipsqueak and the whores and R&R and the fear and the feelings of cowardice and the rage and the hostility toward any Oriental person and the grief and the occasional suicidal ideation and the feelings of having been used and exploited and the USS *Repose* hospital ship and the lack of trust and the irritability and the flashbacks and the suspicion toward authority figures and the Vietnamese kids at the trash dump and the lack of compassion and the survivor's guilt and blowing up gooks and the anger and remorse and the shit-burning details and anything else I can think of. I explain, as best I can, that the rules of normal civilized behavior in war are often suspended and down is up and the bottom is the top and crazy is sometimes a reasonable alternative to sane. I even tell him about the NVA scalp, just as an example of how easy—oh, how very easy—it is to descend, sometimes imperceptibly slow and other times quickly, into savagery. And at other times perhaps even walk that tightrope that sways on the edge of madness. He listens to it all.

After one session, in which I relate the circumstances surrounding obtaining my souvenir body part, he gets quiet and tells me, "If I were you, I would not mention that scalp thing to anybody." The NVA scalp, even after hearing a litany of other horrors, seems especially troublesome to him. Perhaps I should have left the scalp incident out, never even mentioned it in the first place. I was just trying to help him understand. If, in fact, that is remotely possible. After all, I don't really understand most of it myself.

"Why not?" I ask, for I mistakenly think everything is on the table.

"Well," he answers, "I just don't think it would be in your best interest."

Several weeks later he quits working for the Veterans Administration and goes into private practice. I hate to see him go.

I think with a little more time I could help him make some real progress...

Five Days Home

My father and I
sit in the shade
of a chinaberry tree.
Talk softly of the last good war.
A time of ration cards
and Gold Star Mothers.
"A uniform meant free drinks
and a lot more,"
my father says.
"But they kept me training aircrews
stateside...
and wouldn't let me go."

In the lower pasture
a phantom chopper whines.
Rotors thrash hot wind
as it wobbles upward
with another half-dead cargo.
I blink the image away.

"I won't ask if you killed anyone,"
my father says,
"because I don't want to know."
Just as well, I think angrily.
My personal count is a little hazy.

46

A Little Too Cute

"You can't patch a wounded soul with a Band-Aid."—Michael Connelly

"I stopped fighting with my inner demons. We are on the same side now."—Anonymous

"What was it really like?" Clint asks.

Back a couple months from Vietnam, I am now—in drill instructor terms—a "scuzzy civilian" and have a job loading furniture into trucks. Clint is my drinking companion in a redneck bar near the back gate of a nearby Air Force base. In the background, a less-than-mediocre house band is crucifying the Beatle's "Twist and Shout." A friend from high school, Clint is home for good after a college baseball scholarship and a subsequent ruined knee thwarts any and all Major League dreams. Clint is the first person to ask me about the war. In fact, he is the *only* person I can remember asking me anything about it.

I try to come up with an appropriate answer. What was it really like? Maybe, I think, I can relate the last two years to some event with which he is familiar. But I come up with nothing, as there is simply nothing with which to compare it. No way to even begin. And even if I could somehow describe even a small part of the experience, he probably would not believe it anyway.

"Well," I say, "it really was not too bad." Perhaps we can drop the subject and concentrate instead on the single young women gathered in clusters around the nearby tables. Most are lonely wives of deployed airman from the Air Force base waiting for someone to ask them to dance. The more desperate ones, I learn quickly enough, are perched by themselves like timid parakeets on stools by the bar. Their availability is directly proportional to how long their flyboy husbands have been absent. I scan the room for my next potential twisting-and-shouting dance partner.

169

The Body Burning Detail

"Did you ever kill anyone?" Clint asks. Apparently there are a lot of people, especially those who have never been to war, who are interested in the answer to this particular question. A combat veteran will never make an inquiry of this type. It is a noncombatant, war-movie-fantasy-influenced, morbidly curious, obscenely insensitive, scuzzy-civilian question. And so I answer Clint, to the very best of my ability, thusly:

"Yes. No. Maybe. I don't know. Probably. Somebody killed them. I was there. What difference does it make? That was my job. And if I didn't kill anyone I sure tried like hell. Why do you ask? If the actual number is important, it is one ... or two ... or maybe hundreds. Or none. I have no idea." Perhaps the most brutally honest answer is, "It is really none of your business."

Clint sips his beer and contemplates my words. If he is offended by my response he doesn't show it. Maybe he thinks I am just kidding. Although I like Clint, I really don't care much what he thinks. We are worlds apart and I suddenly and surprisingly wish I was back with my Marines on some nameless firebase. This bar scene, full of unfaithful wives and with too-loud background music sung by a raspy-voiced fat guy, is strangely and vaguely depressing. I order another round. A couple more beers may keep this slow and creeping feeling of darkness at bay.

"I wanted to go," Clint muses. "But I had this scholarship and all. Now, of course, with this bad knee I couldn't go if I tried."

How convenient, I think. It seems to me a lot of people with physical disabilities are frustrated Audie Murphy's. Perhaps some of them really do wish to serve. I can't possibly know. But the sad and ironic common element among them is that by having avoided the war, they almost always think they "missed" something...

"You should be thankful," I say to Clint, "that you didn't have to go. Your fucked-up knee is probably the best thing that ever happened to you. Get down on your one good knee tonight and send up a thank-you prayer. You still have both legs and you ain't dead. So you limp a little ... don't sweat the small stuff."

Clint gives me a quizzical look. It briefly occurs to me that I am sounding just a little on the "crazy" side. A lot, much to my astonishment, like Hutch.

Later that night, on the way out of the bar, a young shirtless redneck is challenging people as they walk to the parking lot. There are tattoos over each of his nipples. One says "Sweet" and the other says "Sour." Cute.

170

46. A Little Too Cute

A little too cute for me. Apparently he sees my look of disgust and raises his fists in a fighting stance.

"Do you want some of me?" he challenges. A feeling of uncontrollable rage envelops me instantly.

"As a matter of fact," I reply, "I do." I overpower him immediately, getting to the inside of his flailing fists and putting my hands around his rather skinny neck. On top of him now, my death grip produces a look in his eyes that is best described as kind of a helpless and sudden terror. This is much more than he bargained for. From somewhere far away I can faintly hear Clint yelling my name. A couple of guys then help Clint pull me off. We leave the poor guy on his knees, gasping for breath.

Clint is driving and he is quiet on the way home. The incident has unnerved him and surprised me as well. This is only the second fight, if you can even classify it as one, in my entire adult life.

"You were going to kill that guy," Clint says, breaking the silence.

"Probably," I reply. "He sure acted like he needed killing."

Clint drops me off at my parents' house. I am thinking I need to do some serious reflection on my conduct and attitude. This "rage" thing, which bubbles up unexpectedly and quickly comes to a rolling boil of homicidal anger, can easily get out of control. I need to get a handle on it ... soon. Either that or maybe end up in jail for the rest of my life.

"Call me next week," I say to Clint. "We'll go out again."

That was forty-five years ago. Clint still hasn't called.

47

BLOOD MONEY

"The root of education is bitter, but the fruit is sweet."—Aristotle

"A man who has never gone to school may steal from a freight car; but if he has a university education, he may steal the whole railroad."—Theodore Roosevelt

A couple years or so after Vietnam I am back at the University of South Carolina on a government ride via the G.I. Bill. Tuition is less than five hundred dollars a semester and with my monthly check and a little part-time job, I live modestly but well. Later, I go to work full time and continue to attend school. Ten years after high school, I finally graduate. Better late than never...

In contrast to my miserable previous scholastic performance, my grades are acceptable. For one thing, I stay away from the hard sciences and mathematics (which I have no interest in anyway) and stick with liberal arts courses. English lit, history, sociology, political science, et cetera. Much to my amazement, I find that if I just attend class and read the assignments, the good grades follow fairly easily. Will wonders never cease? The tests are mostly essay exams and my time in the Marines has given me extraordinary skills of producing entertaining and convincing doublespeak. As my old gunnery sergeant would say, "If you can't dazzle them with brilliance, baffle them with bullshit."

Another technique which is especially effective concerns "tuning in" to the professor's individual political persuasion or philosophy and then regurgitating it at some point within the essay-question answers. At various times in my college career, I ascribe to socialism, atheism, liberalism, anarchy, revolutionary theory, pacifism, nihilism, capitalism, and a host of other "isms" which I can't even recall. For the majority of my courses I make A's. Without exception, every professor falls for this seemingly obvious con.

172

47. Blood Money

No one knows I am a Vietnam vet. Although I am a little older than most, my semi-long hair and struggling student persona fool everyone. It is not popular to be a military veteran, especially in light of recent events. The massacre at My Lai, a village in Vietnam where American troops slaughter a couple hundred defenseless Vietnamese civilians, is currently in the news and anti-war sentiment is now somewhere in the stratosphere. The media is continually releasing new details and accounts of the atrocity—each revelation more horrific than the last.

The American Army troops at My Lai were led by a second lieutenant junior-college dropout named William Calley, a short-statured loser who probably should never have been in the Army in the first place. At least not as an officer. He perhaps could have been a competent shit-burning private, but I have my doubts. Where are the company commander and battalion commander as these rapes and murders are being perpetrated on these helpless, unarmed villagers? It's a valid question, but I already know the answer. They are flying safely above the fray in their Huey helicopters, asking for situation reports and body counts. In the end, probably as a result of the massive and far-reaching cover-up, nobody goes to jail.

The photographs in *Life* magazine are especially disturbing to me—desperate Vietnamese mothers, cowering in a ditch, vainly attempting to shield and protect their children from American soldiers gone berserk with bloodlust. The term "baby killers" is more than appropriate here. I simply cannot fathom *my* Marines participating in anything resembling this wholesale butchery. The incident also results in an evaluation of my own coping mechanisms. Perhaps, I conclude, these Vietnamese peasants are not simply "gooks" after all. Maybe they are really just people, with families and dreams, not unlike ourselves.

A political science professor, who is anti-war and extremely bright and convincing, is railing one day in class against the U.S. policy in Southeast Asia. The war is a mistake, he maintains, and the unintended consequences will be far reaching and potentially devastating to our national psyche. An ideology, he says, is an elusive, determined and resilient enemy. I agree with him, as the war has already been devastating to my psyche. This shameless My Lai debacle is especially troublesome. During class, I make several comments which I consider to be witty and insightful, without revealing I am a vet. (In retrospect, the comments are probably more smart-ass, naive, simplistic and unsophisticated, but such is the arrogance of youth.)

A girl in the class, who has previously established herself as kind of a feminist, comments about my remarks after class. She is smart and has a slight masculine vibe going, which is fine with me. She is also cute, opinionated and articulate. We end up talking over coffee. In discussing the "domino theory" of creeping Communist expansion, I state that if the Commies should invade the West Coast, I will wait till they get to Kansas City before taking any action. A dinner invitation is the result, which of course is the intention of all my animated cleverness in the first place. Things are looking up...

At her apartment a few days later, the political conversation continues over wine and baked chicken. She seems to like me and I pick up several cues that I interpret as a precursor to a little "mattress polo" later in the evening. Hope springs eternal. This is the early 1970s, the sexual revolution is still raging, and penicillin will still cure anything.

"Are you on scholarship?" she asks. This is an innocent question, as she is probably just curious how I am paying for school.

"No," I say, without hesitation. "I am getting the G.I. Bill." Her expression darkens.

"You were in the military? Why would you want to do that?" Apparently she is having difficulty reconciling my classroom anti-war status with me ever being in the military.

"Well," I say defensively, "I was drafted. Ended up in the Marines." I don't get into any details, hoping we can drop the subject and get back into something a little lighter. Some playful social chitchat. I don't like the manner in which the conversation is progressing. This may not end well.

"So you were in Vietnam?" Her tone has gone from warm and fuzzy to Popsicle cold. I have the distinct feeling the mattress-polo game has now been forfeited. If in fact it was ever scheduled in the first place.

"It was either that or go to jail," I say. But, as per my penchant for smart-aleck comments that so ill served me in the Marines, I simply cannot leave it alone. Plus, I am getting a little angry.

"Surely," I say after a suitable dramatic pause, "you don't begrudge me my little 'blood money' check every month?" The question is designed to piss her off. Apparently it is highly successful. She does not respond for a minute or so.

"You know," she says flatly, "I don't need this. I don't want this. Part of the reason this country is in such bad shape is that we feel we must send a check to every cocksucker who spent a little time in the military."

"Thanks for dinner," I say as I am leaving.

Other than that, it was a lovely evening.

4 8

POLICE ONLY

"A policeman's lot is not a happy one."—Gilbert and Sullivan

In 1971, prior to shopping malls changing the face and culture of America, downtown Columbia, South Carolina, is bustling and vibrant. Major department stores, theaters, bars and restaurants do a thriving business and streets are crowded with shoppers and soldiers from nearby Fort Jackson. The Vietnam War manpower requirements are still fueled by the military draft and many, if not most, of the young soldiers will end up there in a matter of months. The Southeast Asia killing fields show no sign of drought or crop failure anytime soon.

As a recently hired rookie patrolman, after a brief training and probation period, I am assigned a walking patrol "beat" in downtown Columbia. With the exception of a relatively few cold winter days, the work is easy and pleasant, consisting of loading up drunks in the paddy wagon, sometimes directing traffic, and the occasional shoplifting incident/arrest. When business owners can see you on the street and your radio calls are answered promptly, the beat cop has the freedom to come and go as he pleases. I hang out in pawn shops, movie theaters, restaurants and the bus station. At age twenty-two, there are many young waitresses, shop girls, meter maids, and pretty, single nurses at the Baptist Hospital emergency room—all looking for romance. Or at least a reasonable substitute. I recall those early days with fondness. The pay? One hundred and five dollars a week—before taxes. But after Vietnam, I reluctantly conclude the job is, well ... a little on the boring side. Vietnam, despite the fear, death and chaos, was never boring. But there are worse things than being bored. Being dead, for example.

One walking beat assignment in the warehouse district down by the river is lonely and no fun at all—especially in the winter. Nothing open and no one to talk to, especially on the midnight shift. In those days rookie cops are traditionally assigned a "walking" beat at least a year or so before being assigned to a patrol car. Once, in the middle of the night, I discover a furniture warehouse back door suspiciously open. In checking out the place, I almost shoot myself in a full-length mirror. (The asshole has a gun!)

Sometimes the shift street sergeant will come by and pick me up in his patrol car. An older cop (at least at the time I think he is "old," probably fifty or so), he is fascinated by my tales of R&R in Singapore. While being entertained he drives me around, warm and comfortable in the passenger seat, and subsequently delays my return to the cold and lonely warehouse desolation. If the veteran sergeant ever has doubts as to my stories' veracity, he never indicates it. Once I contemplate making stories up to keep him amused and continue riding me around in the warmth of the patrol car. But that is never necessary—I have enough true ones.

A few times I am assigned as one of two radio dispatchers at police headquarters. Answer the phone, determine the problem, and send the appropriate response. Headquarters is located downtown in a poor, seedy area and people often walk in to report crimes or whatever. A desk sergeant, like one would see in a major city, takes their complaints. Late one afternoon a young black woman walks in bleeding from her throat. Obviously, she had been seriously cut and is subsequently not making a lot of sense. The desk sergeant, who has a terminal case of police burnout disease, looks up casually from reading the afternoon Columbia Record newspaper. He listens for a moment or so before waving her backward with the fingers of one hand.

"You want to step back a little," he says, "you are bleeding all over my paper." I am watching through a little half window that divides the radios from the sergeant's desk. He listens for a few more seconds. She may as well be speaking Mandarin Chinese. The desk sergeant loses patience quickly.

"On second thought," he says, "go stand out on the porch. You are getting blood all over the lobby."

After thirty seconds or so he turns and speaks to me through the window. "Jones," he says in the same voice he uses to order coffee, "you want to call an ambulance ... or something." Then back to reading the afternoon newspaper. A lifetime of witnessing human tragedy has turned off his "compassion" switch. I recall the wretched, desperate and starving

The Body Burning Detail

Vietnamese kids at the Gio Linh trash dump and how little it affected me at the time. Perhaps this inhumane and insensitive response is some sort of psychic defense mechanism. I don't know. The shrinks and academic eggheads can figure it out. I do know that now, many years after the war, it is emotionally difficult to watch television commercials featuring suffering, ill and dying children. I immediately turn the channel.

Walking a beat, my first assigned criminal investigation is at the Greyhound bus station. Someone has broken into one of the pay toilet stalls in the men's room. Since I always wanted to be a detective, this is my chance to showcase my developing investigative skills. (Detectives wear nice clothes, work the day shift, and once they shed the "monkey suit," are instantly superior to their former co-workers in uniform. At least most of them think so.) I write a detailed report of two pages, interview several potential witnesses, and recover several dimes on the bathroom floor. Unfortunately, as of this date, the perpetrators are still at large...

Once, in those early days, I attempt to arrest someone in the middle of a crowd for some minor offense. It is a stupid, rookie mistake and I pay an immediate price. During the fight my nightstick is wrestled away and the new owner proceeds to demonstrate the many uses of this police "baton"—which is really a fiberglass club. After several days in the hospital I am left with a permanently crooked finger as a lifelong reminder of my lack of invincibility. Lesson learned. Any arrest can go south very, very quickly and over the next few thousand arrests I come out undamaged— at least physically. After several years almost all cops, in my view, end up cynical, suspicious and a little paranoid. Older cops have a couple of sayings: Get there firstest with the mostest. (In other words, in any arrest situation gain control and do it quickly.) Also, it is far better to be judged by a jury of twelve than carried to the graveyard by six. Fortunately, I never need to shoot anyone. But I come alarmingly, frighteningly close to dropping a hammer at least two or three times. These incidents, by the way, all involve someone waving a firearm around who is reluctant to follow commands. As in "Drop the gun!" To this day, probably none of them realize how close they were to a long and involuntary dirt nap.

The DeSoto Hotel, downtown Columbia, is known as a local house of prostitution. Fat Albert, a three hundred or so pound black guy, bootlegs a little on the side and runs the place with an iron hand. I never hear of any problems there. Never get a call. No complaints. On the weekends the lobby is filled with young soldiers, all looking for love in obviously the wrong places, waiting to go upstairs. They will not be beaten, robbed or cheated out of their money. The girls stay out of sight. I never, ever see any of them.

Across the street from the DeSoto a steakhouse, Shimmy's, feeds the cop on the beat without charge. A table in the back of the restaurant, marked Police Only, is reserved for this purpose. The only requirement is that the officer traditionally leaves a quarter tip for the waitress. (A quarter? This was a long, long time ago...) The tab is taken care of by Fat Albert and the girls from the DeSoto. At first, being a young and dumb idealist, I am reluctant to participate in what is obviously a payoff of some sort. But after a few months on the job I rationalize it away. Who am I to protest a decades' long tradition? Plus, the steaks are delicious.

The job can be dangerous, but nothing like Vietnam. Much later, one of my former partners is killed in a police motorcycle accident. A shift lieutenant is shot and killed in an ambush-style shooting. A super nice guy who I like immensely, I am pleased and heartened to learn that his murderer is killed by fellow officers in a subsequent gunfight. Perhaps he attempts to surrender ... perhaps not. I wasn't there.

Years later, after graduating from college, I take a job as an undercover narcotics officer in a much smaller department. It is not something I really want to do, but see it as a step toward a detective job. Undercover work is dangerous in perhaps ways unfamiliar to most people. It consists of getting people to like and trust you and then convince them to engage in illegal activity. They are involved in illegal activities anyway, but your job is to convince them to let you join them. After a length of time it is sometimes difficult to determine which side you are on. These are the early days of the dope culture when buying a couple pounds of marijuana gets you thinking you are into Mafia territory. It all seems a little silly now. Eventually, in a roundabout way, it does result in a detective job with the railroad police.

The Military Police have an outpost at Columbia police headquarters and often patrol downtown on the weekends along with the beat cops. Seldom do the soldiers cause any trouble, other than getting drunk and sometimes participating in a little jackassery. Most of these young soldiers, by the time they are allowed in town, respond well to authority figures. I can't remember arresting any of them, but turned several over to the MP's for a trip back to Fort Jackson. I feel kind of sorry for them as I know where many are going... They seem too young and extremely naïve and I resist the temptation to tell them, like my infantry instructor sergeant, that "You guys have no idea." A lot of the MP's stationed in Columbia later come to work for the department after they get discharged from the Army. They all, at least the ones I know, make exceptional cops.

The U.S. Army has a program that pays local cops a twenty-five-dollar bounty for turning in any AWOL soldiers. At the bus station, they are relatively easy to spot—short hair, civilian clothes, military shoes, and no orders.

But for some reason I never find any AWOL soldiers. Not one.

EPILOGUE

"I think there is a false notion that we ought to heal. There is something to be said for remembering."—Tim O'Brien

"So we beat on, boats against the current, borne back ceaselessly into the past."—F. Scott Fitzgerald

And the years go by... Vietnam is peaceful now, some fifty years later, still with a Communist government but economically doing very well, thank you. The United States has diplomatic relations with the Vietnamese and we even have an American Embassy there complete with Marine security guards. Our current involvement is with Iraq and Afghanistan and after some fifteen years of war, both countries are still ... well, Iraq and Afghanistan. The changes in these three countries, despite obscene expenditures of blood and treasure, have been somewhat underwhelming. There is no military draft now and few of our elected officials have ever donned the uniform of our armed forces. Less than one percent of our population is currently serving in the military. It is difficult to put a positive spin on any of this, but there is cause for some hope.

Recently at a writing seminar at a community college, I meet some young veterans of both Iraq and Afghanistan. They are upbeat, cheerful and impressive. Many have completed multiple tours in both "sandpits" and some have serious physical and emotional issues related to their sacrifices and service. But they are moving on with their lives with strength and dignity and no traces of self-pity, remorse or sense of entitlement. I leave the event with a soaring sense of pride and hope. Perhaps our country is not doomed after all. These young veterans, both men and women, are truly America's new "greatest generation."

Once, on a firebase in Vietnam, I encounter a young grunt on the perimeter with an unusual looking rifle. It is a bolt action gun with a long scope similar to a deer hunting rifle. In fact, it *is* a hunting rifle, but the Marine is a sniper hunting North Vietnamese Army soldiers. "This is my second tour," he tells me. "On my first tour I got fourteen confirmed kills." He calls them kills. Not enemy soldiers or people or even gooks. One of his best kills, he says, was a guy running full speed along a rice-paddy dike. "I led him just right," he says proudly, "and he ran another twenty-five yards before he finally dropped." He pauses momentarily at the memory, staring wistfully across the fog-shrouded valley. "I love it," he says finally. "God help me but I love it..." At the time, I remember thinking that someday I need to write a book.

Mac, my fighting hole partner in Vietnam, was killed in action on February 23, 1969. Twenty years later I finally gather enough courage to call his mother. While with the grunts, Mac had picked up a little souvenir NVA rifle cleaning kit. Somehow, after his death, it came into my possession and I thought she might like to have it. The first thing she says is about what you might expect...

"Why," she asks, "did you wait twenty-some years to call?" An excellent question. But I have no answer.

"Well," I reply, "I don't really know. All I do know is that I will never, ever forget him. I can see him laughing now..."

"I always thought he would come back," she says. "In fact, he told me many times not to worry. 'I am coming home.'" There is an audible sigh. I am thinking this call may have been a mistake.

"His dad never got over it," she continues, "and he passed away three months after we got the news."

Mac's mother did not know a lot of details about his death. "Some lieutenant wrote," she says, "but not much else."

Although I wasn't there, I heard from other Marines who were and I tell her what I know. I leave out some details which I think may upset her. Mostly I just talk about how much we all loved the guy and how devastated we were on the day we learned of his fate. On each anniversary of his death, I never fail to think of Mac, age eighteen, his head of blond curls thrown back and his infectious, easy laugh. I mail her the little souvenir. She expresses appreciation and relates she will share our phone conversation with his family. I am glad I called ... I think.

And the years go by... My own son, influenced by my Marine boot camp stories, enlists two weeks after graduating high school. The stories seem to have had the opposite effect of my intent. In 1994, the family attends his graduation at Marine Corps Recruit Depot, in San Diego, California. With the exception that the blatant physical abuse of recruits now seems to be absent, the rest of boot camp appears to be about the same as it was in 1968. When the Marine Corps Hymn is played, it surprisingly stirs a lot of long dormant emotions. My kid looks great in a jarhead uniform and he has already bought into the "esprit de corps" and mystery that is the Marines. As anyone who has been there will confess, it is an easy thing to do.

A few years later, after his first enlistment, he rejoins the Marines shortly after Nine/Eleven and volunteers for the infantry. It is a decision that eventually will cost him his physical and emotional health, his career, and even his family. But does anyone really know how any of our choices will affect us somewhere down the road? For Chase, it seems like the thing to do at the time.

One evening I get a call on a satellite phone from Afghanistan. My son explains that his squad was ambushed and he is flush with excitement, adrenaline and fear after his first firefight. One of his squad is wounded, but will survive. Later, both in Afghanistan and then in Iraq, many more of his friends will not make the return trip home alive. What do you say? I try to encourage him and tell him to look out for the members of his squad and they will in turn look out for him. But he already knows that.

Later that same evening my wife and I go to a local restaurant. A college baseball team is there—young, handsome guys, carefree and bantering among themselves like jocks do. All about the same age as the young Marines in Afghanistan. I feel some resentment towards them and want to tell them that ten thousand miles away, while they are eating hot fudge cake, young men like themselves are hunkering in holes and hoping to see the next morning. It all seems a little unfair... I want to tell them about my friend Mac. And Doc. And all the others...

There is a risk in writing a memoir—especially one that deals with war. People are uncomfortable reading about mayhem and savagery. And perhaps you can't blame them. I wrote some war poems that were widely published and lost a few friends as a result. In shopping this manuscript around I lost one more. But this is not a "tell all" confessional. Some things I have never mentioned to anyone. Not that it is anything of which I am ashamed. It all seemed like the thing to do at the time.

A Union soldier, in a letter home during America's Civil War, perhaps explains it best: "A few of us fellas went down to Gettysburg. A lot of us never made it back. If you weren't there, you can never understand."

INDEX

Numbers in **bold italics** indicate pages with illustrations

185

Index

Index

machine guns 28, 42, 46, 104, 106
Macpherson, Myra 49
mail 11, 29, 43, 62, 66–7, 81, 83, 85–6, 107, 112, 117, 183; distribution 125; to parents 30–3
marijuana *see* drugs
marksmanship 21, 23
Mason, Steve 77
McNamara, Robert 147
McQueary, Rod 5, 45
Medal of Honor 123, 126
medevac 67, 79, 110, 122, 126, 142, 154
Mencken, H. L. 142
mess hall 16–7, 26, 28, 30, 39–40, 78, 104, 143
military recruiters 9–10, 11
Minh, Ho Chi 42
mongoose 141–2
movies 7–8, 15, 92, 132, 144
Murphy, Audie 170
Musashi, Miyamoto 109
music 57, 60, 94–5, 169–70; sixties 132, 153
My Lai 173

napalm 92, 113
National Guard 9
Navarre, Gen. Henri 147
Nietzsche, Friedrich 71
Nixon, Richard M. 60
nuoc mam 135

O'Brien, Tim 121, 181
observation tower 147, 152–3, 155, 159
Officer Candidate School 14
Okinawa 31, 32, 64, 72, 129, 134, 162–3
101st Airborne 36
Operation Prairie 10
Operation Purple Martin 104, *122*

paratroopers 36
Parris Island 13, 15, 27–9
Paycheck, Johnny 39
Pearl, Minnie 46
Pecker Checker 69, 89, 90, 100, 101, 107
People magazine 5
Pipsqueak, Sgt. 139, 142–6, 152, 160–1, 162, 165
platoon 15–6, 21–2, 24, 111, 149
Playboy magazine 107, 117
Post Exchange 129
pot *see* drugs
Prick-25 121

pride 26, 58, 11, 181
Prince Charles 25
prostitutes 131–3, 134–6, 137, 153, 158, 165, 178
"psychic numbing" 157
Puller, Lewis B. "Chesty" 19, 24, 125
punishment 15, 25, 27, 126, 136

Quang Tri Province 10, 39, 44, 62, 126, 128, 136, 139, 142, 144, 151, 158, 160
Quantico 10

R&R 42, 76, 89, 100–3, 126, 134, 160, 165; in Singapore 128–30, 131–4, 136, 139, 177
rangemasters 22
rats 63, 69, 77, 97
Red Cross 142–3
USS *Repose* 142, 144, 165
Riles 104–7, 129
Risk, L. Cpl. *122*
Rivera 58–9, 122, 163
Roberts, Oral 72
Roosevelt, Eleanor 68
Roosevelt, Theodore 172

Sassoon, Siegfried 107
Schmidt, Gary D. 134
search and destroy 7, 149
2nd Battalion 10
Selective Service Board 9, 31
Shakespeare, William 99
Shields, Brook 80
shit *see* human waste
short-timers 135, 154, 156
shrapnel 53, 154
Silver Star 112, 126, 137
Simpson, Vanardo 63
Sinatra, Frank 97
Singapore *see* R&R
snipers 81, 109, 182
South Carolina 9, 11, 13; Columbia 29, 176, 179–80
South China Sea 101–2, 142, 147
South Vietnam 32, 39, 101
South Vietnamese Air Force 78
South Vietnamese Army 93, 147, 149, 154–6, 158
Southeast Asia 9, 42, 97, 134, 147, 161, 173, 176
spiritual experience 122
staging 31
The Stars and Stripes 123

Index